FINDERS KEEPERS

Also by Dee Brestin:

Building Your House on the Lord
Ecclesiastes: God's Wisdom for Evangelism
Higher Ground
Proverbs & Parables: God's Wisdom for Living

FINDERS KEEPERS

Dee Brestin

*Introducing Your Friends to Christ
and Helping Them Grow*

Harold Shaw Publishers
Wheaton, Illinois

Library of Congress Cataloging in Publication Data

Brestin, Dee, 1944–
    Finders keepers.

    1. Evangelistic work.   I. Title.
BV3790.B665   1983   269'.2   83-8522
ISBN 0-87788-259-2

91 90 89 88 87 86 85 84 83 6 5 4 3 2 1

*To Steve
my co-laborer,
my sweetheart,
my friend*

Contents

Acknowledgments

During the last three years I have interviewed Christians who came to know the Lord as adults. I looked for those who had a reputation for a close walk with the Lord. "How did you become interested in spiritual things?" I asked. "How did it happen? What was said? What was done?"

I learned that the Lord's Spirit moves in various ways. I heard Christ's name exalted by Baptists, Presbyterians, charismatics, Mennonites, Lutherans—to name a few. Their stories were as numerous as the people, yet, two principles were evident: the principles of *finding* and *keeping*. These principles are the foundation of this book.

I want to thank all those Christians for opening their doors and hearts to me. Without their stories this book could not have been written. (In a few cases it seemed prudent to change names because of the potential of hurting others.)

I want to thank my editor, Luci Shaw, for encouraging me to write a book on personal evangelism. Her enthusiasm and advice kept me going during the years of interviewing, writing, and rewriting. I am also grateful for Virginia Hearn, whose skills in copy-editing honed this book into shape. I found myself wondering if readers realize just how much help an editorial staff often gives a writer.

Thomas Dunkerton of Compton Advertising gave me guidance in conducting interviews. The evangelism research of James Engel of Wheaton College has been of immense help.

I also am indebted to Greg Scharf, pastor of Salem Evangelical Free Church in Fargo, North Dakota. I have often thanked the Lord for Greg's expertise in the Scriptures and his discerning mind.

Finally, I want to say to my family—my husband Steve and our three children, J.R., John, and Sally—thank you for telling me to do that interview on some nights when I could have been with you. Thank you for fixing your own breakfast on mornings when my writing was going well. Steve has often said that he believes a husband and wife are to be in submission to each other because they are co-heirs in the grace of life. He's shown me again and again that he means what he says.

Thank you, every one of you.

What Happened in Akron— An Overview

Finding:
Making friends with non-Christians and loving them into the kingdom

Keeping:
Teaching those who seem to believe to obey all that Jesus commanded

HAS THE LORD ever used you to bring someone else to Christ? The only comparable experience, in my mind, is having a baby. What a miracle! What joy. I have participated in these two kinds of births and, in both cases, though I knew I was not the creator of life, God used me. The dramatic transformation that takes place in an individual who has received Christ is confirming evidence of a personal God who makes us new creatures in Christ.

Akron, Ohio: 1972-1976
In order to explain the principles of finding and keeping, I want to tell you about four years that my husband Steve and I spent in Akron, Ohio. When we moved to Akron I had been a Christian for only six years, so I could remember vividly what it was like to be without the peace and purpose that Jesus gives.

On July 1, 1972, Steve began a residency in orthopedic surgery at Akron General Hospital. One of the first functions I attended was a coffee welcoming residents' wives. The day was sultry hot. I sat on a blanket spread under a shade tree watching women move about in shorts and sundresses, sipping iced tea with lemon slices. Although I felt a bit intimidated by their sophisticated ease, I knew they were as vulnerable as I. I knew that every person needs Jesus no matter how polished her or his exterior, no matter how seemingly self-sufficient. I wondered how many of these women already knew Him. I also wondered how many, even though not committed to Him, might be interested in coming to a Bible study. Would there be anyone? Would there be a Christian willing to help me start a study? Steve had mentioned that he thought Don Baldwin, a second-year resident, was a Christian, so I decided to look for Don's wife, Mary-Alice.

I got up and began to wander slowly through the clusters of chatting women. I smiled and glanced at name tags. When I spotted "Mary-Alice," I introduced myself. And as soon as we had some privacy, I broached the subject. "Mary-Alice, I'd love to get a Bible study started with this group. Would you be interested in helping me?"

Mary-Alice's first response was to smile warmly, reach out, and squeeze my hand. "I think it would be great, Dee, because there's a real need here. But I've been here a year, and I've found that these women simply aren't interested in spiritual things. I hate to throw a wet blanket on your idea, but I doubt anyone besides you and I would come."

I wasn't going to be dissuaded so easily. Surely out of sixty women, Mary-Alice and I could interest two others. That would give us a start. Reluctantly, Mary-Alice agreed to help me try.

The Club for Residents' Wives then had a September meeting to form interest groups. The person in charge of each group made a short announcement and passed around a sign-up sheet. Right after the groups for bridge and tennis were announced, I stood up. Though my knees were shaking, I smiled as I told them how interesting a beginners' Bible study could be. Then I passed around the sign-up sheet.

Mary-Alice's prophecy had been right. Figure 1 shows how the sheet looked when it came back.

BEGINNERS' BIBLE STUDY
September, 1972

Sign here for an interesting study of the Gospel of Mark! We'll have good discussions over coffee and donuts. Babysitting. Thursdays at 9:30 A.M.

1. Dee Brestin	6.	11.
2. Mary-Alice Baldwin	7.	12.
3.	8.	13.
4.	9.	14.
5.	10.	15.

Figure 1

To add to my discouragement and embarrassment, the lists for the other interest groups were substantial: fifteen had signed up for bridge, ten for tennis, seventeen for arts and crafts.

What was the matter? Driving home I had some bitter thoughts. "Well, Lord, I tried. Obviously these women are just a bunch of worldly doctors' wives. Hardhearted. Interested only in material things. Unreachable."

But deep inside I recognized the Spirit's soft prompting. My attitude was wrong. I hadn't even begun to try. Not too many years before, *I* had been uninterested in spiritual things. What if some unfamiliar woman had stood up and announced a Bible study? Would I have signed up? Probably not. Was it because I was hardhearted and unreachable? When I applied that judgment to myself I was more understanding. The Spirit reminded me that the person who had spoken to me about Jesus was someone I loved and trusted. These residents' wives didn't know me at all. For all they knew, I was some kind of unbalanced fanatic. I realized I had to get to know them and show them I could be trusted.

And so the Lord, in His sovereignty, had me stumble on the principle of "finding." *Finding means making friends with non-Christians and loving them into the kingdom.* It means leaving your cloister and going into the world the way Jesus did, seeking those whom the Spirit might be drawing. It means loving with unfeigned love. That kind of love manifests itself in spending time with a person, doing things that he or she enjoys. That kind of love manifests itself in listening, in responding to needs. In time, that kind of love manifests itself in sharing the gospel of Jesus Christ with them spontaneously, as a result of natural sharing in a friendship.

Finding: September 1972—February 1973

I hadn't signed up for any of the other interest groups because I had felt that, as a Christian, I shouldn't be taking the time for those things. Now the Lord was telling me that, as a Christian, I had better reevaluate that decision.

I tried to recall the women I had met at past coffees. I asked the Lord to guide my memory and thoughts. Lee, a warm and vivacious woman, came to mind. She was hostessing the bridge group that month, so I called her. (I was completely unaware that there were any taboos about that activity among some Christians. It wasn't until we asked Christian friends if they knew how to play bridge and saw their horrified looks that we realized it. But then they proceeded to teach us "Rook" which is essentially the same as bridge.) When I asked Lee if I would still be welcome to join the bridge group, she told me I was an answer to prayer. They had fifteen women and needed one more. I agreed to come Tuesday and then every other Tuesday night for the next year.

Many times that year I questioned my decision to "find." For one thing, I was much more at ease with Christians than with non-Christians. As we played bridge, hospital gossip abounded. I had to fight both the temptation to join in and the temptation to silence them with some "holier than thou" comment. Sometimes I felt as if I had no personality at all—just a great stone face drinking coffee (to stay awake) and examining the cards (to distract myself from the gossip).

I remember one rainy night coming home and sitting in our dark living room. My family was fast asleep, but I, with caffeine running through my veins, would be long in joining them. I began questioning the Lord. "Is this a wild goose chase? Am I really accomplishing anything?" I waited for His answer, and in the still of the night, He spoke to me—not out loud, but within me. "This is right. Seek a closer relationship with Lee and with Ann."

I genuinely liked both of them. Ann and I had coffee together. Lee and I went Christmas shopping. In each I began to see a flicker of interest in spiritual things. Lee and I had several in-depth conversations. I found myself caring deeply about these women. I treasured their friendship.

Meanwhile, Mary-Alice was doing her own finding. She began a Good News Club for the children in her neighborhood. She went around the block inviting the children to a weekly meeting of Bible stories, songs, games, and treats. Through this, not only did the children grow to love her, but she drew the interest of a few of the mothers. Becky and Janice, in particular, grew to appreciate Mary-Alice. Becky told us later:

> Mary-Alice would tell me funny things my kids had said at her Bible club and we'd laugh about them together. I couldn't get over how much she seemed to care about my kids. She was willing to have kids spill Kool-Aid on her rug and track snow through her hall. I couldn't help but be impressed by her attitude.

In autumn 1973, one year after our first attempt, Mary-Alice and I decided to try again with our beginners' Bible study. In addition to standing up before the residents' wives, we personally invited the women who had become our friends over the last year. Figure 2 shows our enrollment.

BEGINNERS' BIBLE STUDY
September, 1973

1. Dee	4. Ann	7. Ava
2. Mary-Alice	5. Becky	
3. Lee	6. Janice	

Figure 2

Why did these particular women agree to come to a Bible study? I've come to believe that the Spirit was drawing them before Mary-Alice and I ever came into their lives. Although it is a mystery, it seems there are times when the Spirit draws some people, but not others. That's why it is so important that we search for those whom He is drawing. If we look for them prayerfully, we'll find them. And once we have found them, it is relatively easy to interest them in spiritual reality. If that is so, you may ask, why hadn't these women responded the first time they were invited? Well, Satan may have convinced them that Bible study was dangerous, or boring, or beyond them, or unnecessary. But the love of Christ, displayed in two weak believers, broke down those barriers.

Lee, for example, had tried to be a good Catholic. She had been faithful in church attendance and obedient to the rules of her church. She had a heart that desired to please God. Later she said:

> I had always felt I loved God, but I could see He was more real, more personal, to you. I wanted that too, but I had been warned not to try to study the Bible myself. But knowing you, Dee, seeing your enthusiasm and knowing how the Scriptures affected your decisions, made me want to try.

A year before, I had judged Lee, along with fifty-eight other women, as being hardhearted and unreachable, yet she wasn't anything of the kind.

I have already mentioned Mary-Alice's neighbor, Janice. A few years before, Janice and her husband had begun seeking God, but fell into the net of a cult, a group that demanded all their possessions and time. Months later, after a battle to get out, they emerged scarred and withdrawn. When Mary-Alice invited Janice's son to her Good News Club, Janice was wary, but gave her consent. Despite her pain, Janice still had a thirst for God. During the next year Mary-Alice's life and consistent love aroused her hope—and so, guardedly, Janice decided to visit our study.

And so we began, the seven of us. As you can imagine, the next six months were exciting. During that time, as we studied first Mark and then Romans, Lee, Ann, Janice, and Becky all seemed to come into a personal relationship with Jesus Christ. By mid-winter new life seemed to pulse in each of those women. Their opened eyes and eager hearts searched the Scriptures with a longing to know God better. They began to invite still others, and by September 1974 our ranks had grown to twelve.

Keeping: September 1974—June 1976

Finding and keeping are not two distinct steps in evangelism, but rather they blend in a continuous cycle. If we separate them, we may fail completely. Finding means making friends with non-Christians and loving them into the kingdom. But of course we can't be sure if people are truly in the kingdom. It can look very much as if a person's profession of faith is strong, but we can be misled. Of course God isn't. He knew who would be His even before the foundation of the world (Eph. 1:3-5). The best we can do is make a calculated guess. That's why we mustn't stop at finding, but move continuously on into keeping.

Keeping means teaching those who seem to believe to obey all that Jesus commanded. It is not our responsibility to judge who truly is a Christian and who isn't. Our responsibility is to teach those who seem to believe to be obedient. When they are showing the fruit of discipleship, we can have some confidence that they have truly been won. By teaching all who seem to believe, non-Christians may discover the truth about themselves and Christians will grow in their faith.

Looking back at the Akron group, I have no idea when each of those women came into a saving relationship with the Lord. It could be that some knew Him before they came to the study, though they may not have fit the evangelical mold. It could be that some who seemed to be Christians were simply adept at picking up the terminology.

Ann was one of the most conscientious women in the study

group. She always completed her lesson and her memory work.
She was intelligent and articulate and she seemed to believe.
Yet, a year after I considered her a Christian, we had an astonishing conversation. I was visiting her in the hospital after the
birth of her son.

"You know what happened to me last night, Dee?"

"You had a baby!"

"Yes," she laughed, "but something else—just as exciting!"

"What?" (I was truly puzzled.)

"I received Jesus as my Savior and Lord. I've become His
child. I'm saved!"

I could hardly believe my ears. I even argued, "But you already knew Him!" She was adamant. She had just become His
child.

How do you teach someone to be a keeper of the Word?
First, you must be a keeper of the Word yourself. Those whom
you are discipling are going to be watching you, imitating you.

In our group we gave homework, asked for memorization,
and continually emphasized personal application. As the
women saw the changes that this discipline brought to their
lives, they were anxious for more. We stepped up the pace. We
gave more homework, memorized longer passages. We also
gave different women opportunities to lead the discussion (no
one studies harder or learns more than the leader).

We did an in-depth study of prayer, using the Fisherman
Bible Studyguide, *Let's Pray Together.* We learned how to pray
with notebooks, being alert for answers. We prayed for each
other during the week. I've often thought the Lord is particularly
quick to answer the prayers of new Christians, perhaps as a
confirmation to them of His reality. As our faith grew in the
amazing truth that the God of the universe is personal, our
prayers became increasingly specific.

We encouraged opportunities for ministry. Mary-Alice orga-
nized a nursing home ministry and several visited with the
elderly, wrote letters for them, and planned elaborate bulletin

boards with thought-provoking displays about spiritual things. Lee spearheaded a group to work with "mobile meals" (delivering hospital meals to shut-ins). Women with gifts of mercy, exhortation, and evangelism began to recognize specific ways they could be used of the Lord. An additional benefit of those ministries was that they were a testimony to the life-changing power of Christ. Other residents' wives noticed. A few more began attending our Bible study.

At what point does a person become a keeper of the Word, a disciple? Obviously it's a lifelong process, but certain signs indicate that the process has begun. Is he showing love to others (even to those who do not love him)? Does she have joy in the Lord? A gentle spirit? Is he less materialistic? Does she have a thirst for the Word, a desire to know God better? Does he have a heart for the lost, the hungry, the suffering? Is she active in a fellowship of Christians? Does he use his gift in a specific ministry?

By autumn of 1975, our family's last year in Akron, there were sixteen in the study. We continued to rotate leadership, now with the vision of preparing individuals to lead future groups.

We were a close group. Drawn together by studying God's Word and sharing our deepest needs and hopes, we experienced a depth of love that the world will never know. My last few months in Akron were filled with bittersweet feelings as I realized how dear these women had become to me.

In April I gave birth to a much-prayed-for little girl. My sisters in Christ presented me with a beautiful quilt. Each woman had taken a square and embroidered a picture and an appropriate verse along with her initials. Interspersed between squares of pink and blue gingham were intricate designs of sunsets, newborn babies, angels, and rocking horses.

In June, Steve finished his residency and took a job at the Seattle Public Health Service Hospital. During the nation's bicentennial, we drove our family across the country to our new

home. With tearful embraces and promises to write, I had said
goodbye to my Akron friends. I took their quilt, and before we
had unpacked anything else, Steve hung it on the nursery wall.
As I rocked our baby, I looked at each of those gingham squares
and prayed for my sisters 2,000 miles away—for Lee, for Mary-
Alice, for Janice, for each one.

Afterward: July 1976—December 1978
Several of us kept in touch. By December 1978, Christmas
cards were bringing exciting reports. Six of the women, inspired
by their experience in our Akron group, had begun evangelistic
studies of their own (see figure 3).

BEGINNERS' BIBLE STUDIES
December, 1978

Becky	**Lee**
group study in Oklahoma	group study in Akron
7 women	8 women
Melinda	**Janice**
group study in Akron	group study in nearby Canton
8 women	10 women
Dianna	**Terri**
group study in Texas	group study in Georgia
7 women	8 women

Figure 3

Some had left when their husbands took jobs in other cities.
Others chose to leave the core group to begin other groups in
the Akron area. Those who had been found and taught to keep
the Word were now finding others and teaching them to keep
the Word.

Summary of Akron: 1972-1978
Over a period of six years, addition had given way to multiplication (see figure 4).

1972:	2 women	Finding: Making friends with non-Christians and loving them into the kingdom
1973:	2 women +5 women <hr>7 women	
1974:	7 women +5 women <hr>12 women	Keeping: Teaching those who seem to believe to obey all that Jesus commanded
1978:	8 women (avg.) x6 leaders <hr>48 women	Finding-Keeping-Finding

Figure 4

You don't have to be a whiz in math to see the potential.

The Lord led me, a step at a time, into the process of finding and keeping in Akron. But it wasn't until I did my interviewing that I realized that what happened in Akron was happening everywhere. Over and over people told me how friends had sought them out, loved them, and shared Christ with them *(finding)*. Over and over, people told me how friends had taught them to obey the Word *(keeping)*.

Jesus and Finding
The principles of finding and keeping did not originate in Akron in the 1970s. They originated with Jesus, in the example He lived for us and in the words with which He commissioned us before He ascended into heaven.

"The Son of Man came to seek and to save" (Luke 19:10). Jesus was a finder, a seeker. He walked miles on dusty roads taking the long route in order to reach out to others. He went to their weddings, He walked by their fishing boats, He lived among them. His life radiated compassion. He fed the hungry and restored sight to the blind. He freed lepers and ate with tax collectors. Although He was often criticized for His intimate involvement with sinners, He was steadfast in His purpose. Because of His lifestyle, He attracted people's interest. Jesus did not stay in the fold of His friends. He consciously went out seeking lost people and loving them into the kingdom.

Is it still true, in the twentieth century, that we need to spend time with those who are not Christians before we can effectively present the gospel? Dr. James Engel, chairman of the Communications Department at Wheaton Graduate School, an expert in evangelism research, summarizes his findings like this:

> Usually evangelism with total strangers is ineffective. . . . Christians must earn the right to share with another person, and this most commonly means that a friendship must be established. . . . Studies of spiritual decision processes frequently show that the most significant influence was someone who cared enough to be a friend.[1]

Obviously there are exceptions to friendship evangelism. I don't want to give the impression that it is only in the context of friendship that God can work. When I began my research for this book and explained to people that I was looking for common variables in evangelism, several warned me I was trying to put God in a box. My dad quoted Montaigne (1533-92) to me:

> We want to enslave God to the vain and feeble approximations of our understanding, him who has made both us and our knowledge. Our overweening arrogance would pass the deity through our sieve.[2]

When I wrote to Thomas Dunkerton of Compton Advertising for advice in conducting my research, he generously gave me advice, but buffered it with the warning that there is no magic formula by which people come to God.

I believe in friendship evangelism, in finding, but I am not going to limit God. I interviewed many people who came to Christ through the influence of campus ministries such as Campus Crusade, and who had spent relatively little time with the person who presented the gospel. What I hope to accomplish is to persuade you that it is a loving and wise act to take the time to nurture genuine friendships. In my interviews I found that most people were wooed and won by someone they knew relatively well. Christians had followed in the steps of Jesus and steadfastly gone out, spent time with someone who was not yet a Christian, and loved him or her into the kingdom.

Jesus and Keeping

In addition to seeking, Jesus concentrated on training twelve men to be keepers of the Word. And among those twelve, He worked even more closely with three: Peter, James, and John. How did our Lord disciple His men? He spent three intensive years with them. He prayed for them. He taught them the Word. He gave them specific assignments. He took them with Him as He ministered to people's spiritual and physical needs.

When Jesus gave The Great Commission, He told us to "go and make disciples" (Matt. 28:19). He elaborated by saying, "teaching them to obey everything I have commanded you" (Matt. 28:20). In the Greek, the word *obey* is, literally, "keep." This is a command that we have not taken seriously. We tend to be satisfied when someone seems to believe. But that is insufficient. Engel says there is

> a non-biblical tendency to define the role of the church primarily around "saving the lost." Evangelism thus takes center stage, with the result that Christian growth is secondary. Anyone with much experience in mass evangelism can point to crusades that supposedly have reached thousands, few of whom ever show up anywhere near the church because of lack of follow-up and cultivation. Perhaps they were converted, but who knows?... One cannot separate evangelism and cultivation and be true to the biblical mandate.[3]

To follow in the steps of Jesus and to be obedient to His Great Commission, we must be concentrating on a few and teaching them to obey, to keep, everything He has commanded. It is vital that we help seeming believers go beyond head knowledge to active obedience. Only then will we be bearing the kind of fruit that will reproduce itself. Only then will we be carrying out the command to make disciples.

Part I

Finding

*Finding: Making friends
with non-Christians
and loving them
into the kingdom*

1

Jesus Makes a Difference

*The greatest favor you can do for anyone,
more than a million dollars, more than a cure for cancer,
is to introduce him or her to the Lord Jesus Christ.*
—Paul E. Little[1]

*I discovered that in my new job I was surrounded by
born-again Christians. I felt like a target, a prize
to be won. And I hated it. They would come up to me and
say "I'm praying for you, Candy." I felt like
telling them: "Get away from me! I don't want you praying
for me. You don't care about me!"*
—Candy, a nurse from a Seattle area hospital

JESUS CHANGES LIVES. I *know* He's changed mine. I've seen Him transform others. His Spirit is moving on this earth, seeking people who are seeking Him.

Yet I was not prepared for the experience I had in researching this book. Armed with microphone and tape recorder, I went into the homes of individuals who had come to know Jesus as adults. They told me how they met Him—and though it might have been five, fifteen, even forty years ago, their eyes might glisten or their voices tremble. We shared a sense of awe at that life-changing power.

I wish you could meet those people. A loss occurs in the transfer from flesh and blood to pen and paper. I feel a little as John may have felt when he began his first letter saying he actually had seen Jesus with his own eyes, touched Him with his hands. Or as Peter expressed it: this is no fairy tale. Jesus was a

real human person. The people I interviewed were real too.
Come with me into their homes.

Charlie and Mary

I interviewed Charlie and Mary early in the evening, before their
children went to bed. Mary's long hair was tied back with a
ribbon and she cradled a tiny baby in her arms. Near her chair
four-year-old Christian worked diligently on a puzzle. On
Charlie's lap a little girl stole glances at me from the security of
her father's lumberjack frame. Charlie is a narcotics investigator.
His muscular body, husky voice, and tendency to take charge
were obviously helpful in his dangerous job. Yet as I listened to
Charlie and watched him stroke his daughter's hair, his tender-
ness came through:

> Mary and I made a pact when we got married: *no children.* That
> was the deal. I didn't want that responsibility and Mary agreed. We
> wanted to be free to drink and carouse.

I was struck by the incongruity between the people who were
being described to me and the man and woman I was meeting.
Charlie continued:

> We were drinking heavily, each running with our own crowd. We
> hardly saw each other. I had a feeling that pretty soon there was
> going to be an end to the marriage—but I didn't much care.

At that time, Charlie's dad died. His dad had been a central
figure in his life and news of his death simply demolished Charlie. At the funeral, Mary and Charlie visited with Charlie's
brother and his wife. Mary told me she couldn't take her eyes
off this couple because they were so changed. Mary said:

> Colleen used to be just like me: hard, uptight, a chain-smoker. Now
> she was so (Mary paused, looking for the right word) . . . *gentled.*
> She was so feminine. Even her hair, once short and boyish, was
> soft and long. I wished I could be like her. I just kept staring at her.

When Mary questioned Colleen, Colleen told her she needed
to make a commitment to Jesus Christ. Colleen said, "Mary,

if you get down on your knees and repent, Jesus will forgive you."

A few weeks later, Mary discovered she was pregnant. When she told Charlie, he felt angry and betrayed:

> On top of Dad's death, that was more than I could cope with. I told her to take care of it—to get an abortion.

Mary didn't get an abortion. She kept thinking about Colleen and what she had told her. If Jesus was real, Mary reasoned, she had better not take this child's life. She began to seek the Lord in earnest. Charlie said,

> Seeing Mary getting serious about the Lord made an impression on me. She didn't see the Lord's business as some hocus pocus funny business. She was talking about it more and more and it stirred something inside me.

Mary began attending Elmbrook Church in Milwaukee. She received Christ and grew in her faith. One day she took Charlie, as he put it, "at gunpoint," to talk to the pastor, Stuart Briscoe. He talked to Charlie about the Lord and about the child, but Charlie didn't seem to respond. Finally, about a month before their son Christian was born, Charlie gave in. His sinner's prayer was "Okay, Lord, you got me."

But the Lord began to work with this, and slowly changed Charlie. When I talked to him, five years later, the Charlie he had described was gone. With a tremor in his voice, he told me:

> Life is so different now. Sometimes I think about how I nearly destroyed a child. I've wasted so many years. I'm making every day count now. We've been so blessed by these kids. We want to raise them to know and serve Jesus. I want so much to help other people. I want them to know about Jesus.

Carol
When I asked Carol on the phone if I could come and interview her, she was enthusiastic. "I'd love to be a part of that. Yes, please come."

The next day I walked up to Carol's home. On the front door was a knocker that said "Peace to All Who Enter Here." I knocked, and a lovely poised young woman opened the door. As Carol took my coat and gestured for me to take a chair at the kitchen table, I noted that here lived a woman with a gift for homemaking. The kitchen sparkled. Cut flowers and a small lit candle graced our table. Fresh coffee was perking nearby. Carol sat down, eager for our interview to begin, so I asked her to tell me what her life had been like before Jesus.

> I was going through a terrible terrible time. My first marriage had failed, and it had been hard on me and the kids. Some hope came into my life when I married again. But now this marriage was going bad. I hated my life. I hated this house. I hated myself.
>
> I was drinking quite a bit then. A lot, really. There would be many nights I would sit in the living room drinking and crying. I wanted a divorce, but how could I put the kids through that again? I'd cry hysterically, and I'd plead, "God, help me!" I didn't know what to do.
>
> Despite all that, I managed to put on a good front. Most people didn't know what I was going through, but my friend Shirley knew. She kept telling me about Jesus.

When Carol asked Jesus to come into her life, He changed her attitude toward herself, her life, even her house. He saved her marriage. A dramatic turnaround? Yes. Jesus can do that.

Al and Joyce
Al suggested I meet him and his wife Joyce at their home for a simple lunch. His teaching schedule at North Dakota State University allowed him a midday break which he often spent with Joyce.

Joyce was tall and lean with salt and pepper hair. Her quiet manner contrasted with the exuberance of her bearded husband. Occasionally she would brush away a tear and smile to confirm Al's words. His story illustrates that people don't have to be at rock bottom in order for Jesus to make a difference in their lives.

I wasn't an alcoholic, I wasn't a criminal—just an ordinary sinner. But still my conversion was spectacular. When that spark was ignited, things began to change. What can I tell you? I understand better the leadership position God would have me take as head of the house. As a Scandinavian I tend to be pretty stoical, and the Lord has really been dealing with me in helping me to be more expressive in showing love to Joyce and the children.

I looked inquiringly at Joyce in an attempt to draw her out. She smiled and said simply, "He's a different man." Al continued,

Our marriage is better, though it wasn't bad. Oh, how I pray our children marry Christians. You have that third Person. There's an excitement, an enthusiasm in your marriage. Our whole perspective about life is different—how can it help but be? We have a personal relationship with the living God!

Betty and Roger

In choosing whom to interview I avoided people who were new in their faith. I wanted to make sure the changes they told me about had stood the test of time. Betty had been similarly cautious about Roger when he came to the Lord. She had considered divorce many times, but each time Roger had persuaded her he would be different. Since they had five children, Betty wanted to believe his promises, but each time she was disappointed. They had been married nineteen years when Betty decided she was going to get a divorce. Roger left, but he desperately wanted his family back. He told me:

I did everything I could think of to persuade Betty to let me back. Promises, pleading, flowers—nothing seemed to soften her. She was determined. She wanted out. She wanted to start a new life. She filed for divorce.

When Roger called Betty's sister for advice, she suggested Roger meet with her pastor for counseling. "I was very unenthusiastic about meeting with a Protestant minister," Roger said, "but, to show my good intentions, I went."

The pastor, in a series of meetings, led Roger into a personal relationship with Jesus Christ. Because his conversion was genuine, there began to be changes in Roger's life. But Betty, understandably, was skeptical:

> I didn't trust him. Friends warned me he was just being nice in order to get us back. It had been so hard to get away, I didn't want to go through it all again. But still, he did seem different.

A few days before the divorce was to be final, Betty prayed. As a little child she had gone to a Baptist church, where she thinks she might have received Jesus. She had wandered far from Him, but now, at this traumatic time, she turned to Him. As she prayed, she remembered a Bible verse, Romans 8:28. "And we know that all things work together for good to them that love God, to them who are the called according to his purpose" (KJV). Betty couldn't remember who had taught her the verse, but she suspected that it had been during her visits to that Baptist church more than thirty years ago. Then it occurred to her that she didn't need to put her trust in Roger, she could put her trust in the Lord. She called Roger and told him she would go to church with him.

Attending a Christ-centered church together, both grew in their faith. Roger had always wanted to be a good husband and father, but he hadn't been able to live up to that desire. Now he did better. Betty and Roger hadn't wanted to argue in front of their children, but before they couldn't help themselves. Now they had help. I talked to one of their sons. Ron told me:

> They used to always be yelling. So many arguments. Everybody was upset a good part of the time. But now Mom and Dad are different. Somehow they aren't so strong-willed anymore; they are much gentler and kinder.

The fruit of the Spirit is love, joy, peace . . . gentleness. Those aren't qualities we can drum up in ourselves. Rather, they are gifts that come when the Spirit is in control of our lives. For the past six years Betty and Roger, who recently celebrated their twenty-fifth anniversary, have had a rich marriage in Christ.

Though transforming our earthly lives wasn't the main reason Jesus came, it was part of His mission. Jesus wants to bind up our broken hearts, replace our despair with praise, transform our lives into something beautiful.

Beyond This Life

Jesus makes a difference in eternity. No one likes to think about death, but ignoring it doesn't make it less real. Despite all the progress of modern medicine, our life span is still close to seventy or eighty years (as Moses said in Psalm 90). Every person dies.

To think about my own death or the death of anyone I love is difficult. Ecclesiastes, however, says that we should think long and carefully about death.

> "It is better to go to a house of mourning
> than to go to a house of feasting,
> for death is the destiny of every man;
> the living should take this to heart."
> (Eccles. 7:2)

Many of the people whom I interviewed started seeking God in earnest after the death of someone dear to them. René's young husband was killed in an auto accident.

> My mother-in-law came over right after we found out. She ran to me and we held each other. The very first thing she said was, "Oh, René, was he saved?" That was the question that haunted us. While he was with us we had never talked much about God or eternity. Death never seemed like a possibility.

One of the reasons we shrink from thinking about death is that, lurking behind it, is an even more difficult reality: the wrath of God. J. I. Packer has said:

> [the] modern habit throughout the Christian church is to play this subject down. . . . The subject is taboo in modern society, and Christians by and large have accepted the taboo and conditioned themselves never to raise the matter.[2]

Is it right to be silent? The Scriptures are not. Throughout the Old and New Testament we are warned that the day of God's wrath is coming. One day our Lord Jesus will be revealed from heaven in a blazing fire. "He will punish those who do not know God and do not obey the gospel of our Lord Jesus. They will be punished with an everlasting destruction" (2 Thess. 1:8-9).

Jesus used imagery about hell that makes us shudder. It is a place where the "worm does not die, and the fire is not quenched" (Mark 9:48). Four times in the Gospel of Matthew alone, Jesus described hell as a place of weeping and gnashing of teeth.

Packer thinks one reason why Christians won't raise the subject of God's wrath is their feeling that wrath is somehow unworthy of God. Our problem, Packer says, is that we are seeing God in man's image. Human wrath is often partly irrational, self-indulgent, and ignoble. God's wrath is not like that.

> God's wrath is a right and necessary reaction to objective moral evil. God is angry only where anger is called for. Even among men, there is such a thing as righteous indignation, though it is, perhaps, rarely found. But all God's indignation is righteous. Would a God who took as much pleasure in evil as He did in good be a good God? Would a God who did not react adversely to evil in His world be morally perfect? Surely not.[3]

The fact of hell's existence and the prospect of a day of God's wrath do not mean that God is not loving. It was God's love that caused Him to give His Son to be the payment for our sins. The central reason Jesus came to earth was to rescue us from the coming wrath (1 Thess. 1:10b).

All of us choose whether or not we will respond to God's love in Christ. If we do, it will make the difference for us in eternity. The Bible tells us: "Whoever believes in the Son has eternal life, but whoever rejects the Son will not see life, for God's wrath remains on him" (John 3:36).

Our responsibility is to encourage people to face reality. Death is real. God's holiness and His just wrath are real. Christ came as the means of reconciliation and God "has committed to us the message of reconciliation" (2 Cor. 5:19). How can we be silent when we know such an important truth?

Do you care about the people around you who have not received Jesus? Do you believe that they are without hope, without eternal life? Do you want to help them find the One who makes all the difference? The fact that you are reading this book may be an indication that you do care.

Jesus makes a difference in this life and in eternity. Why aren't most Christians sharing that news? I've come to believe that our main problem is the same problem that plagued Jonah.

Compassion: A Missing Ingredient?
I can't think about the book of Jonah without recalling Elva McAllaster's poem, "From Jaffa":

From Jaffa, Jonah once set sail
To find himself sole cargo bale,
In a submarine with a muscled tail.

Coward and rebel, determined to fail;
Slack to obey, and pitched over the rail;
Chagrined when his preaching was found to avail.

Jonah from Jaffa: blood brother we hail. [4]

Jonah's sin was disobedience. When God told him to go and tell the people of Nineveh to repent, Jonah ran the other way. We're often like that, too.

Why did Jonah disobey? You might expect him to say: "I was afraid" or "I didn't know what to say" or "I've been so busy I just didn't have time." But listen to the reason Jonah gave after he had finally been to Nineveh and had reluctantly preached to the people and they had repented. Jonah was displeased. He became angry.

"O Lord, is this not what I said when I was still at home? That is why I was so quick to flee to Tarshish. I knew that you are a gracious and

compassionate God, slow to anger and abounding in love, a God
who relents from sending calamity" (Jon. 4:2).

In other words, Jonah was saying "I don't care about these
people. I didn't want them to come into a right relationship with
you. And I just knew, O Lord, that if they repented you would
forgive them."

Jonah despised the Ninevites because of their cruelties. He
failed to realize that their sinful lifestyle was due to their separation from God. (What would your lifestyle be like if you didn't
know the Lord?) Jonah had no compassion for the Ninevites.
He had known the Lord for a long time and had forgotten what
it was like to be without light and without purpose. (Do *you*
remember?)

The real reason we aren't consistently sharing the gospel is
that we lack compassion for non-Christians. That is the root
cause behind all our other excuses.

Caring Enough to Share

Radio pastor Charles Swindoll helped me recall what it was like
when I was a new Christian. He asked, "Remember when you
first became a Christian? You would lie on your bed thinking
'Whom can I tell?' " That's exactly how it was for me. I was
highly motivated to share my faith, and I was motivated for the
right reason. I cared. I would look at individuals and realize they
were wandering aimlessly in the darkness which I too had so
recently known. I wanted them to come into the light. I cared
that they were missing abundant life in Christ.

One of the most interesting patterns I noticed in my interviews was the high percentage of people who had been led to
the Lord by new Christians. Why, I wondered, are new Christians so fruitful, when they lack both maturity and knowledge?
Then I realized that, in addition to having a ready-made set of
unbelieving friends, they care enough to share. They are so excited about the change in their life and they care so much about
other people that they just can't keep the good news to them-

selves. They run out and tell their friends and neighbors, "Jesus changed my life." They are sincere, spontaneous, compassionate. They are speaking up, and for the right reason. Somehow people know if you are talking to them because you care or because you simply want a scalp for your belt. It's not enough to pretend to care.

Cold-hearted Witnessing

Candy resented the Christian nurses at her hospital because she felt they didn't care about her as a person. When individuals sense that lack of personal caring, they deeply resent your witnessing. (Wouldn't you?) Candy did come to know the Lord, but it was through the influence of one of her patients, a man whom she felt genuinely cared about her.

We do need to be bold, but our motivation, our attitude, must reflect love and compassion. As Em Griffin expressed it, "People bruise easily." If they have been repeatedly or badly bruised, they may become "immune to a more comprehensive and sympathetic presentation of the gospel later on."[5]

Most adult converts come to the Lord through the witness of a friend. Yet, I don't want to make you hesitant to witness to a stranger. If your motivation is right and the Spirit is leading, you should obey. I heard testimonies from people who had responded fully to Christ after the witness of a stranger, but they were aware, even in that brief contact, that the witness came from a person who cared deeply. We must not be compulsive or cute in our witnessing. Our motivation should spring from authentic concern for that particular individual.

Keith Miller said we need the Master's second touch (see Mark 8:22-26) so that we see human beings not as trees walking, but as people who do not have new life in Jesus and are therefore without everything that matters.

If you have been a Christian for a long time, your eyes, like mine, may have grown accustomed to the light. Or if you received Jesus as a child and have loved Him and served Him ever since, it's going to be even harder for you to appreciate

the darkness in which non-Christians live. You've barely experienced that darkness, and so it's difficult to empathize.

There's a book in the Bible, Ecclesiastes, given to us by God
to help us who tend to be cold-hearted. It's a book too often
neglected by Christians, but it can warm our hearts and open
our eyes.

Try This:
● Do the following exercise in your next quiet time. Write down ten specific
ways that Jesus Christ has brought meaning to your life. Then pray over your
list in praise and thanksgiving.
● Begin each day this week with the expectant prayer: "Father, open my
eyes and help me to see the people around me as they are, as individuals
who need love. Show me specific ways to get closer to some of them." You
might remind yourself of this assignment by putting a note on your refrigerator.

2
Ecclesiastes Present-Tense

Most men lead lives of quiet desperation.
—Henry David Thoreau

A PROFOUND BOOK tucked away in the Old Testament, Ecclesiastes, has been largely overlooked by evangelicals. Yet, ironically, it is basic to evangelism. Ecclesiastes can help us understand the hidden thoughts of our unbelieving friends, and, in so doing, can rekindle our compassion. The central figure of Ecclesiastes is "the Preacher" (or, in Hebrew, *Qoheleth;* Ecclesiastes is the Greek equivalent of *Qoheleth).* Qoheleth is a desperate man. He tries valiantly to fill the void in his life with various things "under the sun" only to conclude that nothing in this world gives lasting joy or satisfaction. He plunges hopefully into various pursuits only to crawl back disillusioned and crying, "Vanity, vanity—all is vanity."

There is more than one facet to Qoheleth, and he can teach us many lessons. But he is, in part, a man who is trying to find meaning apart from a personal encounter with God. Thus we are given a Spirit-illuminated look into the hearts of non-Christians. Isn't it time we tried to find Ecclesiastes in our Bibles?

Qoheleth's Frame of Mind
Ecclesiastes begins with a description of Qoheleth's state of mind. He looked at everything under the sun, that is, the visible

things on this earth, and said, "There is nothing of lasting meaning here."

> "Generations come and generations go . . .
> What has been will be again,
> what has been done will be done again;
> there is nothing new under the sun."
> (Eccles. 1:4a, 9)

One man I interviewed shared the thoughts he had, in his pre-Christ days, at his grandfather's funeral:

> When they buried my grandfather, my dad was there, I was there, and my eight-year-old son was there. It was such a gloomy scene. I remember thinking: "Gramps worked so hard on his farm all his life. Now he's gone. What does he have to show for his life? Dad will get the farm and he'll work hard and die and pass it on to me. What's the use of it all? One day we'll all be six feet under."

Qoheleth cried, "There is nothing new under the sun!" In other words, as he looked at life, he couldn't see any permanent meaning. He wanted direction in life, purpose, but he didn't know where to find it. Many of the people I talked to described what it was like before they found Christ. Sandy, a quiet and gentle young woman, said,

> I was living in California alone. I had no family there. I was terribly depressed—unsure of the future, unsure of where I was going, unsure of what life was all about. I doubt that most of the people around me had any idea how desperate I felt. I remember going and sitting in an empty church, silently crying out to God for answers.

One day Sandy noticed a book on a co-worker's desk, Catherine Marshall's *Beyond Ourselves.* Her co-worker lent it to her, and through it Sandy found a personal relationship with Jesus Christ. She also found the answer to Qoheleth's plea, "Show me something *new* under the sun." Sandy discovered that "If anyone is in Christ, he is a new creation; the old has gone, the new has come!" (2 Cor. 5:17).

Ecclesiastes is a prophetic book in the sense that its haunting yearning questions prepare the way for Jesus. Figure 5, taken from my Fisherman Bible Studyguide on Ecclesiastes[1], illustrates Qoheleth's frame of mind.

The Preacher of *Ecclesiastes* cries:

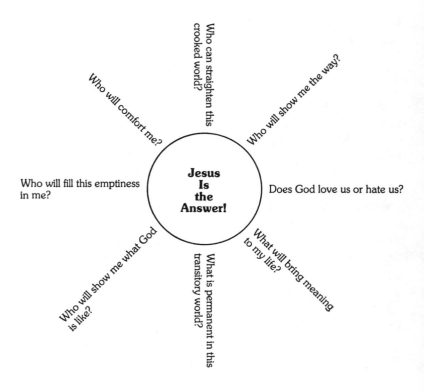

Figure 5

Many non-Christians around you have an outlook similar to Qoheleth's. They have questions, but they feel alone in their confusion. They hide their unhappiness with busyness and superficial smiles. "Even in laughter the heart may ache" (Prov. 14:13a). Research has shown that most people will not reveal their inner longings to strangers, but they will open up to someone who shows them empathy and genuine friendship. Non-Christians will reveal their hearts to us if we are willing to go further than superficial relationships.

Even if you have been a Christian since childhood, there probably have been times when your walk with the Lord has not been close and you have experienced some of the emptiness and purposelessness of Qoheleth. Magnify that many times, and you'll feel part of the ache of those who don't know the Lord at all.

Before I met Christ I was an unhappy young wife. I had so many of the feelings of Qoheleth. I carried a burden of sin on my shoulders—and the only way I knew to deal with guilt was to repress it, or try to. I was in a two-bedroom apartment with a colicky baby all day and all evening while Steve was at med school. I wanted more out of life than folding diapers and scrubbing floors, but I didn't know how to get it. People told me how lucky I was to have Steve and our son, and I'd agree with them. But inside I'd think "I don't feel lucky. What's the matter with me?" I'd have coffee with the other women in the apartment building, and they would chatter on about trivia. I did too. But in the afternoon I'd come home and think "Doesn't anybody else hurt? Doesn't anybody else want more from life than this?"

I remember one day when two other women and I got together to paint and shellac Easter eggs. They were gossiping and laughing, while I was inwardly screaming: "Are moments like this going to be the *high* points in my life? Is life simply a series of dull activities punctuated by an occasional dinner out or the painting of an Easter egg? I *hate* this." But outwardly I was smiling, and painting.

Qoheleth's Search: Worldly Wisdom

Despite his frame of mind, Qoheleth was not ready to give up. His first attempt to bring meaning to his life was through worldly wisdom. He studied the thoughts of the great philosophers. He looked to science and observed patterns in this life. He perceived that life is not fair ("The race is not to the swift or the battle to the strong"). Life is cruel ("I saw the tears of the oppressed"). What was the solution? Who had answers? Qoheleth found that no one had answers. He felt he'd wasted his time, that his pursuit had been "like chasing after the wind." The more you know, the more you hurt.

I talked to a few people who had tried to find meaning in life through worldly wisdom. Ann, now pursuing a career in Christian counseling, told me how much she desired answers:

> Even in high school I was aware of an emptiness in me. Emily's words in Thornton Wilder's play *Our Town* provoked my thoughts. She died and looked back at earth and said, "We never realized life while we were living it." I felt I wasn't realizing life, I was missing something. I read a lot, but I didn't find answers. I remember doing a paper on T. S. Eliot's poem *The Hollow Men,* a depressing piece depicting the spiritual emptiness of people in the twentieth century. Even though at sixteen I didn't feel my life was really hollow, when I looked ahead to future years, to middle age and beyond, it frightened me. It made me want to know if there was a God, if He was really there. If I found out there wasn't, well, then I would adjust my life accordingly, but I wanted to know. When I went to college I was still seeking. Whenever there was a discussion in the dorm, I would be there. But nobody really had any answers, just opinions.

Qoheleth's Search: Wine

When Qoheleth found that the great minds of the world had no answers, but only more questions, he turned to something else. He tried "cheering himself with wine." Many people I interviewed had turned to drugs or alcohol to fill their emptiness. But instead of making them happy, too often it became an addictive and destructive habit. Instead of finding freedom, many of these

people became slaves of the flesh. One man, now the principal
of a Christian high school, said:

> I was twenty-eight, married, hooked by booze, and thoroughly
> miserable. My life was a mess, but I didn't know about any better
> life. No friend had ever shared Christ with me . . .

Qoheleth's Search: Wealth

Qoheleth planned and built a great estate, complete with
orchards, fountains, and elaborate gardens. His parties sur-
passed those of his contemporaries. Any material possession he
wanted, he got. "I denied myself nothing my eyes desired; I
refused my heart no pleasure." In all that, he found "some
delight," yet at the end of the day he was still aware of a great
void. He asked, "What is my life really accomplishing? What
have I gained that will last?" He realized that "Whoever loves
money never has money enough . . . This too is meaningless."

Jan, a doctor's wife from Tulsa, told me,

> At thirty-six years old I was depressed. The money, things, children,
> home, husband, clubs, cars, and cleaning women couldn't give me
> the utopia I had always wanted and expected.

Qoheleth's Search: Pleasure

Qoheleth had a harem. If there was a woman he wanted sexu-
ally, he took her. But that didn't fulfill him. One woman told me,
weeping:

> I was sexually loose in high school. I wanted so desperately to be
> loved, and I confused sex with love. But instead of feeling loved,
> cared for, and fulfilled, I felt almost hated. Girls whispered about me
> and exchanged glances as I walked down the hall. Guys turned on
> me. They'd be so sweet and then they seemed to despise me.
> They'd treat me like dirt. I guess that's what I was—it took the
> blood of Jesus to cleanse me.

Our world is pleasure-oriented. "Grab all you can," we're
told, and most people do. Most of the men and women I talked

to had tried to find fulfillment through money and sensual pleasures. Howie told me about his experience:

> During my junior year in college I went to Aspen with some of my friends. At first, we were having a great time on the slopes—and in the evening we would come down to a condominium where we would dine on some geese and ducks we'd shot the previous fall. I figured that this was the ultimate in life. However, by about the fifth day of that ski trip, I asked myself, if this is the *ultimate,* why do I feel so empty?

A few years before, Howie had heard a presentation of the gospel and had partially responded.

> I left my friends in Aspen, flew into Denver, and checked into a hotel. I wanted Christ to be the Lord of my life. I called a couple of ministers whom I found through a friend in Denver and asked them to meet me at my room. They spent about four hours with me. I made a commitment of my life to Christ at that time and there's never been any question as to the priority of Christ in my daily life since.

After college Howie worked on Campus Crusade staff for a few years. Now he heads a company that helps underdeveloped countries improve their agricultural methods. What would have happened to him if he had never heard a presentation of who Jesus is and why He came to earth? What if Howie had never been told that Jesus wants a personal commitment from us, a relationship with each of us? When Howie recognized the void in his life, would he have realized that it was a spiritual void?

Confronting that void, some people turn to drugs or alcohol to anesthetize themselves. Some fall into numbing patterns of working, watching television, eating, and sleeping. Others commit suicide. And some, because of a Christian friend's bold and loving witness, turn to Jesus Christ.

Enter Despair
After all his pursuits failed to fill his emptiness, Qoheleth
despaired. "All his days [were] pain and grief; even at night his
mind [could] not rest." He hated life.

Are all non-Christians unhappy? I'm not going to try to con-
vince you that all people who have not committed their lives to
Christ are miserable. Many more than we realize *are* hurting.
But Qoheleth was not always unhappy. When he was pursuing
a dream, though it was an illusion, he had hope and was relatively happy. Though individuals may be aware of some emptiness, they feel that as soon as they marry, or as soon as they
own a home, or as soon as they graduate, they will be happy.
For them, the dream lies ahead.

Perhaps we don't feel as much compassion toward these
people as we do toward those who have discovered that their
dream is empty, but we should. When Jesus saw the *crowd,*
"he had compassion on them, because they were like sheep
without a shepherd" (Mark 6:34). All the people we know, even
if they are not feeling desperate, need Jesus. They need Him
in this life. They need Him in the coming day of wrath. People
who are pursuing a false dream may not be as interested in
spiritual things as those who are at the end of that dream, but
someday your words about Jesus may come back to them.
When they are ready, the Holy Spirit may remind them of
something you said. Or someday, if they feel they have a friend
in you, they may turn to you.

Not all the men and women I interviewed were at the end of
their rope when they came to Jesus. The following people are
examples:

Jim: I wasn't really unhappy with my life. But as I got to know Larry
something began to happen to me. His great love for Jesus made a
mark on me. I began to wonder if I was missing something.

Meredith: I wasn't seeking, but my sister planted some questions
in my mind. She made me realize that I had better decide who
Jesus was. If He was a liar or a lunatic then I could continue to

ignore Him and not fear the wrath of God. But if He really was who He claimed to be, I would be foolish not to commit my life to Him.

Lolly: My life was going well. I was experiencing success as a dancer, yet I had times of loneliness. I met some Christians who offered me a different kind of friendship than I'd ever had before. My conversion was very gradual, but their friendship was the beginning.

Even people who seem happy need Jesus. They may not realize that there is a better life. But if they meet you, and see your life, they may be drawn to your God.

If you suspect that someone is hurting, it is wise to give that person priority over a "happy pagan." But often we don't know who is hurting until we get close.

People want meaning in life. Ecclesiastes says, "God has set eternity in the hearts of men." Or, as Pascal put it, "In every man there is a God-shaped vacuum." In her successful book *Passages,* Gail Sheehy recorded that people are afraid. In each stage in their lives, often with increasing desperation as they grow older, they hurry "to pursue their own definition of a meaningful existence so that life won't become a repetition of trivial maintenance duties."[2] Some people are more aware of a vacuum during particular "passages" in their life, but all have that vacuum.

Try This:
- 1 Peter 3:15 tells us to be ready to give an answer for the hope that is within us, with meekness and fear. Be able to give at least one clear presentation of the gospel. (You can find help in chapter 8 of this book.) Memorize the verses. Get them down smoothly. In a world filled with questions, Christians shouldn't stammer.

3
Finding Time for Others

*Sometimes I feel guilty that I'm not involved
in the lives of non-Christians. But I am serving the Lord.
I'm raising these three children to love Him. Isn't
that a ministry? If I had more time, I'd do more. But I'm
involved in two Bible studies with Christian
friends, I'm in church three times a week, and I have a family
and a house to care for. That's all I can handle
right now without going crazy.*
—a woman from Pennsylvania

MOST OF US LEAD BUSY LIVES. It's difficult to find time to develop relationships with non-Christians. But as I interviewed person after person who explained why he or she didn't have time to develop friendships with non-Christians, I began to sense that something was very wrong.

I sympathized with the reasons, but I began to wonder what kind of impact Christians can be having on the world if we are limiting our friendships to other Christians. Have we really been gripped with the realization that God wants to use us to bring the message of reconciliation to a dying world? There must be something wrong with the priorities in our lives if we don't have time for others.

The Christians who confessed feeling guilty about their uninvolvement with non-Christians also seemed to feel that their time shortage was temporary. As soon as they finished school, or as soon as their children were older, or as soon as their job demands eased up . . . *then* they would have time. The problem with such reasoning is that at each stage of our lives we are best equipped to reach others in a similar stage. Students are most effective with students, young mothers with young mothers, and so on. If we wait until that stage is finished, we've missed a God-given opportunity. One nineteen-year-old bride said:

> I regret that I didn't take a stronger stand for Christ in high school. I stayed close to my church friends instead of reaching out. I realize now I missed a great opportunity. Now most of my classmates have gone off in different directions. Those few whom I still see when I go home see me as an old married woman, a world apart from them. And I am. I missed it.

Is it possible we are being deceived by the father of lies when we plan to get involved next year? The writer of Proverbs says:

> "Do not withhold good from those who deserve it,
> when it is in your power to act.
> Do not say to your neighbor,
> 'Come back later; I'll give it tomorrow'—
> when you now have it with you."
> (Prov. 3:27-28)

How can we have time for our families and for our church and still have time to develop a few friendships with those outside? I believe a solution exists, but before we look at it, let's look at two common problems: materialism and church meeting mania. These may or may not be problems in your life, but if they are, it's important to recognize them and take action.

Materialism

Dr. James Dobson has said that the greatest enemy of today's family is time pressure and fatigue. We are so on the run and then so exhausted, we simply don't have time or energy to develop meaningful relationships even within the family. The same problem keeps us from developing relationships with non-Christians.

Dobson feels that materialism is at the root of our overscheduling ourselves.[1] If a family is struggling to keep up with inflation, their solution is to work more hours, either through moonlighting or having both parents work outside the home. Adopting a simpler lifestyle is rarely considered.

Dorothy Pape, returning from the mission field, was struck by how little time North American Christians had—because of their desire for a larger income. She noted that Christian camps were desperate for volunteers because most teens and college students were working. She lamented that fact because she believes that more lives are influenced for Christ in Christian camping than perhaps any other way. But instead of encouraging their college-age children to volunteer at camp, parents encourage them to get paying jobs.[2]

Many doctors make well over one hundred thousand dollars a year, yet feel the need to moonlight in the emergency room to meet their expenses. It is evident that if we let our desire for things control us, there will never be enough money.

Many couples live on less than twenty thousand dollars a year. These families are committed to a simple lifestyle. They want to be able to give time to what they believe is most important in life: people. They have decided not to set their hearts on material things. I find these couples impressive. They aren't listening to the world; they are keeping pace with a different drummer. They don't live in poverty. Their homes are warm and often creatively lovely. Their children aren't hungry or in rags, and often they show some of the character more indulged children lack. These are families who invite people over often, not for steak but for homemade soup or popcorn. They aren't ashamed of their simple way of life. They know in their hearts they have their priorities straight.

When my husband Steve was seeking a Christian medical practice, we visited with two Mennonite doctors, one in Kansas and another in Iowa. Meeting those Mennonite families and seeing their lifestyle has had an impact on our perspective. Both families had consciously chosen a simple lifestyle over an affluent one in order to have more time and money for the Lord. I'd like to tell you about John and Margie.

Margie invited me over for lunch on the spur of the moment. As I drove up to a compact ranch home, I wondered if I had scribbled down the wrong address (aren't doctors supposed to have big houses?). But it was Margie who opened the door, looking fresh and cheerful. Despite the fact that she wasn't wearing makeup, she looked pretty. (The first time I visited a Mennonite church and noted the women's scrubbed faces I felt like a loose woman. I retreated to the rest room to wash off my blush-on and lipstick.) Margie took my coat and I found myself talking easily as her eager questions coaxed me on. My eyes wandered over their living room. The grasscloth and pictures from Algeria reminded me that they had spent a few years in a mission hospital there. The room had warmth and character; its inexpensive simplicity was refreshing.

We sat down to a nicely set table and had Campbell's soup and canned peaches. Margie had had short notice, but that didn't stop her from inviting me for lunch (it might have stopped me if I had been in her place). Her priority was to meet me and develop a friendship, not to impress me.

Margie did impress me, but not in the way the world desires to impress. I was impressed by her attitude toward "things." She was not self-conscious about her simple home or her simple lunch—there was not one word of apology. I doubt that it even occurred to her how differently I was being entertained than I had been on other job-hunting luncheons.

As we ate, Margie and I visited. She told me about several of her neighbors with whom she had developed friendships. She had a thriving evangelistic study going; more and more women from her block were coming. I could see why. Mennonites like John and Margie have an important lesson to teach the body of Christ.

One Thanksgiving we drove across Nebraska with other Mennonite friends, Lorma and Dave. I played a tape for them in which the speaker claimed that since we are children of the King, we should trust Him to bless us with the best in homes, clothes, sports equipment, and so on. Lorma turned the tape off and said evenly, "What this man is missing is the beauty of a simple lifestyle. He has no appreciation of what it can mean to be free of cumber."

There's no doubt about it. If we have smaller homes, fewer clothes, simpler meals, we'll have more time. Will we be miserable? Hardly. Jesus said: "Watch out! Be on your guard against all kinds of greed; a man's life does not consist in the abundance of his possessions" (Luke 12:15). Of what is our life to consist? Jesus tells us that our relationship with God and our relationships with people are to be the first and second priorities in our lives. They are what give us joy, not the size of our income or the size of our house.

There is a freedom, a joyous humor, in the lives of Christians who are practicing Christian simplicity. I like the way John Alexander put it in Doris Longacre's practical book *Living More With Less,* "About half the time when people ask me what's the reason for simple living, I say, 'It's more fun.' "[3]

Church-Meeting Mania

Another time gobbler in the lives of many Christians is what I label church-meeting mania. I mean meeting together with other Christians too many times in any given week. Let me clarify, lest I be misunderstood.

I am solidly behind Christians being active in a local church. The Word clearly tells us not to neglect assembling together. In fact, it is often in the worship service or Sunday school that we gain strength to go out into the world. I am also convinced that we each are to discover our gifts and put them to use in our local church. Some should be teaching, some should be organizing a church library, some should be visiting the sick, and so on. We can't and shouldn't be trying to do it all, but each should be doing something specifically in line with his or her gifts.

Having said that, I also believe it is vital that we limit the amount of time we spend in fellowship with and ministry to other Christians so that we have time and energy to develop a few friendships with non-Christians. One step we can take is to ask for the cooperation of our pastors and local church governing boards. A wise pastor will make a conscientious effort to limit the number of meetings that everyone is encouraged to attend. He will also see the importance of holding workshops on the gifts of the Spirit in order to help members discover their individual gifts and find a specific ministry. This is the way the body of Christ was meant to function—each part doing something, not a few trying to do it all.

Some churches set aside a day of the week where there will be absolutely no meetings in order to encourage "family night." Families are encouraged to spend that evening together, strengthening their bonds. How about another night in which members are encouraged to get to know their neighbors and other acquaintances? How about a night for personal rest and relaxation?

Church is important. Christian fellowship is important. But if it swallows us up so that we are ineffective in the world, it is working at cross purposes with the Lord.

A Better Way

It's easy to schedule all kinds of things in our lives that have no business being there. It's easy to be too busy to listen to the Lord's "still small voice." I have fallen into that trap more than once. I have trouble sitting quietly before the Lord in the morning, seeking His direction for the day. My problem is I have my own plans for how I want to serve Him that day, and I don't want to be given conflicting orders. Isn't that kind of thinking ridiculous? Didn't I give my life to the Lord? Doesn't He know better than I what's best?

Perhaps you think you are obeying the Lord when you are up to your ears in church activity. But unless the instructions for your activity are from the Lord, you may actually be working against His desires. What irony! Is it possible that the Lord wants you to develop a friendship with a few non-Christian acquaintances, but you have been too busy to hear Him?

It is also possible to be involved in good things such as making craft items for Christmas gifts, growing a garden, or learning to scuba dive—and be displeasing to the Lord. The Lord may lead us into any of these things, but the key is to seek His will for each day rather than running off on our own.

I appreciated Charles Hummel's observations about Jesus in his pamphlet, *The Tyranny of the Urgent:*

> The Gospel records show that Jesus worked hard . . . Yet His life was never feverish; He had time for people. He could spend hours talking to one person, such as the Samaritan woman at the well. His life showed a wonderful balance, a sense of timing . . . What was the secret of Jesus' work? We find a clue following Mark's account of Jesus' busy day. Mark observes that 'in the morning, a great while before day, He rose and went out to a lonely place, and there He prayed.' . . . He prayerfully waited for His Father's instructions and for the strength to follow them. Jesus had no divinely drawn blueprint; He discerned the Father's will day by day in a life of prayer . . . *God impresses on our minds the assignments He wants us to undertake* (italics mine).[4]

The psalmist put it this way: "Your hands made me and formed me; give me understanding to learn your commands" (Ps. 119:73). To me this means "You created me, Lord. You have allowed me to have particular weaknesses and particular strengths. Your Spirit has gifted me uniquely. You placed me in a particular life situation. I am the only one with my particular set of relatives, neighbors, and acquaintances. So you know how I could best serve you. Please help me to discern and obey."

Try This:
● Examine your lifestyle prayerfully. Do you have time for non-Christians? If not, what dramatic changes could be made? Discipline yourself, beginning today, to sit quietly before Him in prayer. Put aside your preconceived plans and wait patiently for *His* orders.

4
Seeing the People in Your Path

No one on the lane of some twenty-two families
phoned or called in person to welcome us to the community.
We have been here a year and have only a nodding
acquaintance with the neighbors—and not all of them.
—a woman from Darien, Connecticut[1]

When we moved from Colorado Springs to Fargo
we asked the Lord to put us in a specific neighborhood
where we could be used. So when Marlis came
over with cookies, I was very alert to her. . . . She was so
different from the Marlis I know today. She had
on sweatpants and a sweatshirt and she seemed tired. There
was a futility in her attitude. As we visited, I
sensed unhappiness in her family situation. We discovered
we went to the same denomination, but I didn't
think, from the way she was spending her time (soap operas,
etc.) that she was a believer. It seemed to me that
the Lord had put Marlis in my path.
—Barb, the neighbor who led Marlis to Christ

WHEN I WAS CONDUCTING a small workshop on evangelism in Seattle one man commented: "I live with Christians, I work with Christians, I worship with Christians. With whom am I supposed to share my faith?" Many Christians feel the same way.

It is quite possible that some Christians truly don't have much contact with non-Christians. Those individuals must take specific actions to increase their contact: join an exercise club, become involved in local government, volunteer at a nursing home. Nobody has to live in a Christian cloister, and we certainly weren't intended to do so. Jesus prayed we would be *in* the world.

Most of us, however, already have God-given opportunities

for meeting non-Christians, and we need only to open our eyes and see those opportunities. We will see the people God has already placed right in our path.

My respect for God's sovereignty has increased dramatically as a result of my interviews. I knew, theologically, that it is God who first draws us toward the gospel. Jesus said, "No one can come to me unless the Father who sent me draws him" (John 6:44). Paul tells believers that we were chosen in Christ before the foundation of the world (see Eph. 1:4). That's what I knew intellectually. But as I listened to people's stories, excitement filled my heart. I heard again and again how God had undeniably begun touching their lives. Take, for example, Helen's story.

Helen is a home economist, hostess of a local television talk show. As she tells her story, notice all the ways God drew her to Himself.

In 1971 my mother died after a battle with cancer. I loved her very much and her death turned my thoughts to God and eternity. I think it is very often through death that we discover what life is all about

Like Helen, many of the people I interviewed had lost someone close shortly before their conversion. When someone dies whom you love deeply you long to know what has happened to them and if you will see them again. It was amazing to hear how frequently, at this receptive time in a person's life, Christians came onto the scene and began to talk about Jesus and eternity.

Helen continued:

At work I became friends with Karen. We weren't terribly close, but I liked her. When she took a new job, I missed her. I didn't hear from her for quite a while, but one Easter she called me and asked how to prepare a ham. In the course of our conversation, I asked her what was new in her life. She surprised me by saying she had met the Lord. I was interested, and I asked her questions about how it happened.

Helen and Karen began to see more and more of each other and often talked about spiritual things. Helen began to read her Bible, but put off making a commitment. The following Easter she became very ill, "so ill," she said, "it scared me."

> I think, now, the Lord allowed me to go to the depths for my greater good. I remember reaching for my dusty old Bible on the nightstand and reading Psalms. I think that was the beginning of my commitment.

Like many of the people I have talked to, Helen made a commitment with her heart before she fully understood the gospel. At that time Helen received a call from the local Christian Women's Club.

> They asked me if I would be their "special feature" speaker and do some type of cooking demonstration. I accepted, and that was my introduction to this special group of mature Christians. After my presentation I sat down and listened to the spiritual part of the program. The speaker was a missionary and her testimony moved me. She explained the gospel clearly. I responded silently when she gave an invitation.

I asked Helen if her friend had given her name to the Christian Women's Club. She looked surprised and said no. It had been God who had led the Christian Women's Club Board to call Helen.

One question I often asked in my interviewing was this: "Was there one significant person who led you to the Lord?" The usual response to that question was negative. The people were more aware of a series of events, a series of people in their lives, than of one particular person. I liked the way one woman answered me. She said, "No, not really. God surrounded me!"

It is an amazing thought that the God of the universe actually reaches out to specific individuals and persistently draws them to Himself. Again and again I heard how the Lord persevered in touching some person's life.

One man told me that three people—his doctor, a neighbor, and a friend—offered him the same Christian book in a month's time. The book? *The Gospel According to Peanuts* by Robert L. Short. Although Charles Schulz's faith is reflected in his cartoon characters, that is certainly not a book high on my list of evangelistic tools. *Mere Christianity* or *Born Again* certainly, but *The Gospel According to Peanuts?* The Lord, however, either in His sense of humor, or because He knew that this book was right for Jeff, led three people to recommend it. By the third recommendation, He had Jeff's attention.

Recognition of God's sovereignty should help open our eyes in faith to people already in our path. It might not be coincidence that a neighbor with a child your child's age has moved in across the street. Perhaps you should see some significance in the fact that your old friend Tom keeps coming to mind. God is more in control of our lives than most of us ever realize. Being aware of this will make us expectant. Paul Little said he never knew anyone effective in personal evangelism who didn't have an attitude of expectancy toward the people he met.

Marlis told me that before she was a Christian she was terribly lonely. On one of those lonely days, she decided to "try" praying for a friend to move into the empty house across the street. A month later a family moved in. Marlis took cookies over. She said:

> Meeting Barb is an experience I'll always remember. There was something so special about her. I remember she was excited that I was a Presbyterian. Nobody had ever been excited about my being a Presbyterian! I didn't understand her but I did like her and I even thought, "I'd like to be like her someday." It occurred to me that maybe God had heard my prayer. If there was a God.

When Marlis prayed for a friend, her faith was small. But God heard and responded to her prayer. He sent Barb to her neighborhood. What if Barb had been too lacking in awareness of God's sovereignty to pay much attention to Marlis? Barb suspected the hand of God and worked on developing a friendship with Marlis. In time, she led Marlis to a relationship with Jesus Christ. Marlis is now a lecturer in Bible Study Fellowship and radiant in her joy for the Lord.

Do you remember Mordecai's famous words to Esther? "Who knows but that you have come to royal position for such a time as this?" (Esther 4:14b). Who knows if your life circumstances have not been engineered so as to bring you into contact with someone who is open to Him?

Keith Miller has commented that many active American churchmen, in order to participate in an evangelistic endeavor across town, must first stumble over the bodies of their wives and children and people in their daily paths.[2] I believe that people in your life right now are there because God caused them to cross your path.

People with Whom You Share a Bond
As you develop an expectant attitude, you will become aware of many people with whom you have something in common. Perhaps you live in the same neighborhood or work at the same company. Perhaps you both love tennis. It's possible that God in His sovereignty has given you this common bond. It's at least worth investigating that possibility.

Your neighborhood. Consider the people in your neighborhood. At one time in our society, neighborhoods had a sense of intimacy. People moved into a house and stayed there for fifty years. They knew their neighbors, and their neighbors knew them. Today we have become "a nation of strangers." More than a fifth of Americans move every year, and our rootlessness is increasing. There was a time when oldtimers on a block would invite newcomers over for supper. Now so many are new that nobody takes any initiative toward them. Why bother? Next year they may be gone.

My husband Steve and I are representative of that mobile population. In the last fifteen years we have lived in seven states. I have found that the best way to get to know my neighbors is to take the initiative myself. I am shy, easily intimidated, but Christ has provided me with the boldness to go and knock on my neighbor's door and say, "Hi—I'm your new neighbor. My name is Dee, and I just wanted to meet you." I have always been invited in and warmly welcomed. A lot of people miss those days when neighborhoods were meaningful, and usually they will warm up if you break the ice.

Or you might give an evening or weekend neighborhood coffee. You might limit it to your immediate neighbors, or those who can come on the spur of the moment, or those of your own sex. Since your goal is to get acquainted, you don't want the group to be too large. Invite them in person; don't send a note. Tell them the purpose is simply to get acquainted. Plan a conversational game. Since almost everybody is basically insecure, if left to themselves they may talk only to their spouse or to the one neighbor they already know. Though there may be mock protests at a game, silently, they'll thank you.

One conversational game is called "The Thread Trick." Pass around a spool of thread and ask your guests to break off a certain amount. Then, when all have their varying lengths of thread, explain that they are to wind the thread slowly around their finger until it is all used up. As they are winding, they are to talk about themselves. They may tell about their family, job, goals in life—anything to help others know them better. Most people love to talk about themselves and will secretly enjoy this attention.

How about setting a goal for yourself of inviting one neighbor over for a simple supper or coffee each month? So often we love to have our sisters and brothers in Christ over, but we neglect others. Do you remember what Jesus said?

"When you give a luncheon or dinner, do not invite your friends, your brothers or relatives, or your rich neighbors; if you do, they may invite you back and so you will be repaid. But when you give a banquet, invite the poor, the crippled, the lame, the blind, and you will be blessed. Although they cannot repay you, you will be repaid at the resurrection of the righteous" (Luke 14:12-14).

Invite the physically *and* the spiritually needy for dinner. In his book *The Friendship Factor,* Alan L. McGinniss comments that "It is no accident that so many important encounters occurred between Jesus and His friends when they were at table. There is something almost sacramental about breaking bread with another."[3] When Jesus ate with "sinners," when Peter ate with the Gentiles, it caused a stir of protests. But they were saying by their actions, "I love this person. He is worthy of my having a meal with him."

When I am invited to someone's home, I feel complimented. It is often in the relaxed atmosphere of after-dinner coffee that meaningful conversation takes place. In *Open Heart—Open Home,* Karen Mains tells how the Lord linked her gift of hospitality with her husband's gift of evangelism:

> We soon began to function as a team, working hand in glove. I can't count the times when, with the room softened by candleglow and our hearts by the Spirit, our conversation has lingered into the wee hours with someone finally bowing head and heart before his Savior.[4]

It's possible the first time you meet with a neighbor the conversation will turn spontaneously to spiritual things. If he or she seems genuinely interested, then let the conversation flow. If, on the other hand, they seem hesitant, put them at ease by talking about the subjects in which they are interested. Don't force a spiritual conversation, but don't be afraid of one either.

Get to know the children in your neighborhood. You don't have to have them over for dinner—a Coke will do! Or simply walk outside and play basketball with them. Children love attention from adults. One Christian man we know is so popular with the children in his neighborhood that they come to the door and ask his wife, "Can Mr. Schuster come out to play?" This man has been a tremendous witness to the families in his neighborhood. They want to know what makes him so caring and loving toward kids that aren't his.

Teenagers, though self-conscious, will also respond to genuine interest taken in them by an adult. Do you remember from your own adolescence how rare it was for an adult to talk to you in-depth, to care about your thoughts and opinions? I do. Those who made the effort were really special to me (thank you, Miss Kolander, wherever you are—and thank you, Miss Krepsky).

Spouses of Friends. Another group of people with whom we share a bond are the not-yet Christian spouses of friends. Because of our friendship with the Christian partner, we have a God-given entry into developing a friendship with the non-Christian mate. Doesn't it seem we have a responsibility here? Shouldn't part of bearing another's burden include praying for and witnessing to his or her spouse?

B. J. Thomas, the singer who had us all humming "Raindrops Keep Fallin' on My Head," was a drug addict and, as he put it, in an "impossible, hopeless situation." When his wife Gloria became a believer, she enlisted the help of her Christian friends. She asked B. J. to come home from his travels so he could hear from her and her friends about something that had happened. He told her he wasn't coming home. But, B. J. said,

> Two days later I was home. Gloria and a church full of people were praying for me and I didn't really stand a chance at that point. I walked into this guy's house and I felt the same peaceful feeling and I saw the same glow around his wife and kids. Something was sort of telling me in my mind that I was going to find my way out. When Jim finally got home that night, about 11:30, I was really ready to hear what he had to say. He started telling me about the Lord and telling me about Jesus. [5]

B. J. found the Lord. He was delivered from his drug addiction, and he says that now, most mornings, as he looks in the mirror, he's his own best testimony to the power of Jesus Christ.

In one of my women's Bible study groups, several of the women had husbands who weren't Christians. We prayed and planned for several months to turn our women's group into a couples' group. We began with a potluck (a good one) and a lighthearted get-acquainted session in which we asked each person to reminisce about their first meeting with their spouse. The evening was very positive, filled with laughter. Near the end, my husband stood up and described the upcoming beginners' study for couples we were planning. He invited them all back. Most came and several of the men came to know the Lord.

Non-Christians who share your interests or talents. Another group of people likely to cross your path are the people with whom you share an interest or a talent. Has the Lord given you a love for golf? Are you a bookworm? A hand-crafts lover? A fisherman? Consider the possibility that God gave you this interest so that you would be able to relate to others who share it. Let me tell you about Miriam, a young Christian woman who loved to play soccer. She told me enthusiastically:

> I got this idea for organizing a women's soccer team that would have some spiritual aims. I prayed about it and asked the Lord to give me some assurance it was from Him and not just some crazy idea of my own.
>
> I prayed for a coach and sixteen women. Twenty-four women signed up, including four Christians. We were on our way!
>
> I systemized a prayer plan. Each month one of the Christians prays for three specific non-Christians on the team. We are also paired off as Christians and pray for each other. We pray that our lives will overflow with love. We confess our sins to each other and pray that our walk will be a testimony.
>
> It's been great. We are all getting close to each other. First we have the natural bond of soccer. There's the camaraderie of a team —shared victories, shared losses. And we have time to talk. There's all that time riding to and from the games. We have the rare chance to talk without kids interrupting. Lots of times the talk is about soccer. Sometimes there's a natural opportunity to talk about spiritual things, sometimes there's not. But I definitely feel this is of the Lord and we are moving in His will.
>
> One of the girls hurt her leg last month and several of us visited her in the hospital. As I was leaving, she took my hand and said, "Miriam, you'll never know how much the lives of some of these women mean to me."

I love to read, so it seemed natural, when we lived in Indianapolis, to organize a book club. I invited two Christian women who were also readers and we all invited our neighbors. About twelve of us met to discuss a book we had all read the previous month. The "hostess of the month" chose the book, and we read a wide variety, Christian and secular. I remember discussing Catherine Marshall's *Christy* and Eugenia Price's *The Burden Is Light.* I also remember a wild discussion over atheist author Ayn Rand's *Fountainhead.*

If you don't know many non-Christians, consider joining a group with whom you share an interest. Perhaps you'd like to get involved with a local pro-life group or a nuclear freeze group. Too often Christians think that their only responsibility is evangelism. I don't think you can make a scriptural case for that (Jesus ministered to the hungry, the sick, the afflicted). There is an important link between social and evangelistic endeavors. Christians who go out into the social sphere find more people in their lives and are also viewed as more caring persons than Christians who seem solely concerned with spiritual needs.

Go out into the world. Get to know the people with whom you already share a neighborhood, a friend, or an interest. As you are moving out, be particularly alert, as Jesus seemed to be, to individuals who are part of "the fertile field."

Try This:
• Before you leave for a PTA meeting, an office dinner, or a walk around the block, develop the habit of kneeling or pausing and asking the Lord to direct your attention toward someone He is drawing.
• Take Alan McGinniss' advice: "If you wish to promote stronger relationships with more people, invite someone different to lunch every week or offer to meet people for coffee before work."[6]

5
The Fertile Field

*Do not live like the rest of mankind, who pass
through the world like straws upon a river, which are carried
which way the stream or wind drives them.*
—Susanna Wesley

ALL AROUND US are men and women who are looking for change in their lives. "The fertile field" is a term used to describe people who are seeking. According to Dr. James Engel,

> Common sense would argue that the best audience for evangelistic efforts are . . . seekers, who represent the fertile field. They should receive a greater emphasis in strategy than those who are not so open, all things being equal.[1]

Many of the people I interviewed came to the Lord at a time in their life when they were unhappy, restless, desirous of "something new," like Qoheleth in Ecclesiastes. Perhaps something they had hoped would fulfill them had failed. Perhaps they were in the midst of a traumatic experience such as the death of a loved one, a divorce, or a major personal injury. My research and that of experts has shown that these people are *likely* to be receptive to the gospel if it is presented lovingly and empathetically.[2]

To some people this may sound manipulative. I don't see it like that at all. In the first place, these people are in need of help. If someone is going through deep waters, they're thankful for a lifeline.

Steve and I are saddened by the high number of hospital chaplains who don't know the Lord. They sit by the bedsides of dying patients and talk to them about their wills. Or worse, they give them false assurance. Here are people who truly need to be prepared to face God. Other people who go to marriage counselors may be told that their differences are irreconcilable. We know there is a lifeline that can help all these people, and that lifeline is Jesus. Christians need to be looking for people in need so we can reach out with that lifeline to them.

Another reason I don't believe that this strategy is manipulative is because I believe in God's sovereignty. It's at least possible that He allowed something traumatic to happen to a person because He knew it would make that one consider Him seriously. As Paul said, "Yet we believe now that we had this experience of coming to the end of our tether that we might learn to trust, not in ourselves, but in God who can raise the dead" (2 Cor. 1:9 PHILLIPS).

If a traumatic event is likely to make someone receptive to the gospel, doesn't it make sense that we should present it then instead of waiting until that person's heart hardens again? We should always make clear people's central problem: they are separated from God and need the Savior for reconciliation with Him. When that central problem is solved, Jesus is also there to shepherd us through peripheral problems.

As I listened to people's testimonies I thanked God for the boldness of those who clearly presented the gospel at a time when each non-Christian's heart was tender. Tom and Pauline recognized that kind of need when they received a desperate call from a teenage neighbor, Valarie. Valarie had come into a personal relationship with Jesus and was active in the youth group at Tom and Pauline's church. Valarie's parents were not Christians and were not interested in spiritual things. As Valarie's dad told me later: "I had no need for God. I was totally sufficient and in complete charge of my destiny."

But one day Valarie's sixteen-year-old brother came home with the news that his girlfriend was pregnant with his child and he planned to marry her. Valarie watched her parents' world crumble. Her dad, always strong, sat down, put his head between his hands, and began to cry. Valarie came over, put her arms around him, and said, "It's easy to pray, Daddy."

As she began to pray her dad's heart softened toward the Lord. Then Valarie called her Christian neighbors, Tom and Pauline, and asked them to come over. Too many Christians, when faced with a situation like that, would try to bring comfort without the Savior. Pauline gently yet boldly presented the gospel, and Valarie's parents responded.

How do we find people in the fertile field? There are two ways. First, simply watch for them. Second, consider working in a ministry that deals with a high proportion of tender-hearted individuals.

Watch for People in the Fertile Field

We have a merciful God who cares about all people. We also know He reaches out to those who are seeking Him. Therefore, if we as believers ask God to draw our attention to those who have tender hearts, He will do that.

I interviewed a student from the University of Washington whom the Lord used to lead several other students to Christ. When I asked how he found them, he emphasized that many people on campus are terribly lonely. They have lunch in the cafeteria by themselves, and they walk from class to class alone. He said:

> I recently made friends with a Japanese student who had been totally ignored. He came quite readily to our Christian fellowship, and he responded eagerly—I'm sure partly from loneliness.

In our mobile population, many people are lonely. When we lived in Seattle I would often put our little girl in the child's seat on the back of my bike and peddle over to Kerry Park, my favorite lookout on Queen Anne Hill. In one panorama you could see the Seattle skyline with the Space Needle and the Kingdome; the harbor with tug boats and ferries moving out into sparkling Puget Sound; and best of all, Mount Rainier, looking almost unreal in its immensity and perfectly rounded shape. One day I arrived at the park to find another mother there with her toddler. My Sally and her little boy began to play together on the steps. They chased each other around the water fountain, giggling and chattering.

As I watched them and thought about striking up a conversation with the little boy's mother, I was reminded of a comment made by a missionary friend from Saudi Arabia. He said, "People in America don't really know how to be friendly. We have such great freedom of speech here, and yet people can't even seem to open up a conversation." I decided I wasn't going to be like that. I began by asking this mother questions about her little boy. It wasn't long before Annie was telling me she was new to Seattle and was feeling somewhat homesick. At that point I invited her for coffee the next day and she readily accepted. Annie was part of the fertile field, very open to spiritual reality. I discovered her simply by being alert. There's a good chance there is someone new in your neighborhood, someone who is feeling friendless and isolated.

It is difficult to uncover human needs unless we have first built a bridge of friendship. As James Engel says, "Needs are rarely uncovered in the fleeting contact provided by 'cold-call' evangelism."[3] People who are really hurting tend to build walls around themselves so that they won't be hurt even more.

When Steve and I moved into one home, I had trouble warming up to the woman across the court. She seemed bitter and critical. I judged her unfairly instead of seeing her as a woman who was desperately hurting. Mary was a mother with three children, and she had cancer. I didn't know that. I didn't try to get close to her. I didn't try to understand her. I didn't even invite her to the Bible study in my home because I thought her caustic attitude would ruin the atmosphere. One day the Lord kept bringing Mary to mind. I couldn't believe He wanted me to invite her to our study. I remember praying: "I don't think she belongs at this study, Lord, but if you *really* want me to invite her, have her call me" (she had never called me).

The phone rang. It was Mary. She said, "What are all those cars doing in front of your house every Thursday morning?" I invited her to our Bible study and she accepted immediately—with gracious appreciation. She came, and her earnestness and sincerity touched the heart of every other person there. She affected the atmosphere of our group, but not in the way I had imagined! Mary came to know the Savior that year and flowered into a beautiful woman of God. When she died the next year, we grieved over her death but took comfort in the knowledge that she was ready to meet her Lord. One day we would see her again.

I'm not proud of the above story. I would rather tell you that I reached out to Mary because I had the discernment to see her pain. But I hope I've learned the importance of building a bridge of friendship to people even if they seem cool and indifferent. I'm reminded of Jesus' admonition that if we love only those who show love to us, we are no different from pagans (see Matt. 5:46-47).

Ministry with the Tender-hearted

A second way to find people in the fertile field is to begin a ministry with a section of population which has a high proportion of tender hearts. Two general categories of people with tender hearts are, first, children and youth, and second, people in crisis.

Children and youth. Nineteen out of every twenty individuals who become Christians do so before they reach the age of twenty-five,[4] yet we tend to ignore the young in our paths. Howard Hendricks on his radio program "The Art of Family Living" said:

> You know, we're really not too smart. We put 85 percent of our efforts where we will get 15 percent of the results—and we put 15 percent of our efforts where we will get 85 percent of the results.

I think often of a ninety-year-old neighbor on Queen Anne Hill. Miriam sits for children, cuddling them on her lap, loving them with lemon drops, back rubs, and songs about Jesus. She patiently teaches them Scripture verses until they can say them proudly and word perfect. Why aren't there more Miriams among us? At the Lausanne Congress on Evangelism it was stated:

> We are not really convinced of the desperate need of the third of mankind that is most open to the gospel, and out of whom the world leaders and the authorities of the future will arise. What if the Communist leaders of today had been converted when they were still children?[5]

Perhaps we are reluctant to throw ourselves into child evangelism because we are unconvinced that children's decisions for Christ will bear lasting fruit. What happens to the children who have no support, who perhaps even face opposition, at home? Let me tell you a few stories to encourage you.

Bea, a foster child who spent her childhood in a series of temporary homes, never felt she had roots. She quickly became cautious about getting too close to her current family since she suspected she soon would be moved. She was never in a Christian foster home. When she was five years old, however, a neighbor invited her to Sunday school. That day Bea heard the "House Heart" story, dramatizing Revelation 3:20: "Here I am! I stand at the door and knock. If anyone hears my voice and opens the door, I will go in and eat with him, and he with me." Bea recalled:

I could hardly wait to open the door and let Jesus in. And I knew, from that day on, that though I didn't have an earthly father, I did have a heavenly Father.

All during her childhood Bea found a way to get to Sunday school. She went alone, but she went. A woman now, actively serving the Lord, she is an artist with two shops on the Seattle waterfront. Her paintings of soaring gulls and sunlit landscapes reflect the glory of One she knows intimately.

Others whom I interviewed had come to know Christ in their youth but received no support at home. Some of those individuals drifted far away, yet in their adult years came back.

Barb received Christ at fourteen through a Young Life Camp in Malibu. Her parents opposed her activity with Young Life, feeling she was limiting her friends to too small a sphere. After college she wandered far from the Lord, living what she termed a "selfish, immoral life." From the age of twenty-three to thirty she dated a series of worldly men who made her life miserable. Then, like the prodigal son, Barb admitted that her life was a mess. She prayed, "Please, Lord, give me a good husband." One week later, Dave, Barb's future husband, came into the library where she worked. The two of them hit it off immediately, had a date the next night, and not too long after that were married. As newlyweds, they bought a house from a private party. As they were signing the papers, the former owners asked Barb and Dave if they'd found a church. They hadn't, but both were interested. The woman recommended theirs. She said,

> Our church is a little bit different from the traditional church. We don't have a full time pastor—in fact we have a different speaker every week (it was a Plymouth Brethren Fellowship). Why not commit yourself to coming for six weeks? Then, if you don't like it, go ahead and try something else.

Barb and Dave decided to take her advice. Barb had been strengthened in her faith by the Lord's gracious answer to her prayer for a good husband. And Dave, though not a born-again

Christian, was interested in finding a church where the fruit of the Spirit was evident. (He didn't express it that way at the time.)

Dave tells, with obvious affection, of the man who shook his hand as they walked into Evergreen Bible Chapel. He was warm, loving, and godly. That Sunday, Dave, at thirty-four, heard the gospel explained for the first time in his life. Two weeks later he committed his life to the Lord and Barb recommitted her life. When I talked to them recently, they were on their way to work with World Radio Missionary Fellowship in Europe. Barb told me that her parents, who opposed her involvement with Christians in high school, now enthusiastically support the commitment Dave and she have made.

Does evangelism with youth bear lasting fruit? I liked the way Barb put it: "The Lord in time watered the seed planted long ago." Children and young people are often open to the Lord. Yes, it's more difficult when there's lack of support at home. But the Shepherd is watching them and He's not willing for the wolf to snatch them from His hands.

It's important that we disciple children who come to faith. Perhaps if Barb had been discipled better at fourteen she wouldn't have wandered from God as she did. But the failure in her case was not that she came as a child, but that she was not discipled. Proverbs 22:6 comes to mind: "Train a child in the way he should go, and when he is old he will not turn from it." That isn't a promise—Proverbs aren't promises, but general truths—but, it is generally true that if we present the gospel to children and train them to live godly lives, when they are old they will faithfully serve the Lord.

There are probably children in your neighborhood who would be delighted to come to a weekly children's Bible Club. What child doesn't love stories, songs, games, and treats? If you want help from an organization, there's a good chance you'll be able to find Child Evangelism Fellowship in your phone book.[6] They have meetings to provide ideas and encouragement. If your neighborhood has too few children, they'll find you a neighborhood brimming with children.

Many of my interviewees came to know the Lord during high school or college. In the past I had felt vaguely uncomfortable about campus ministries. I had the impression that these groups would haphazardly go and hit people over the head with the gospel, letting the bodies fall where they may. But since I've listened to people tell how they heard the gospel during their college years, I've changed my attitude. Every person I talked to told me that he or she had been approached gently and cautiously.

Ron's story was typical. He told me that for weeks Campus Crusade advertized the fact that they were bringing André Kole, an illusionist, to the campus. Ron and a friend went to see him. Ron said,

> The first part of Mr. Kole's presentation was basically entertainment, though there were hints of something deeper coming. During intermission Mr. Kole explained that the second part of his presentation would be spiritually oriented and that those who didn't care to listen didn't have to stay.

Even though Campus Crusade had a ready-made audience, they allowed, even encouraged, those who weren't interested to leave. And a few did. At the end of the show, after presenting the gospel through the use of illusion, Mr. Kole asked people to fill out audience-response cards. Again, Campus Crusade was being cautious. They wanted to follow up on those, and only those, who were interested. Ron turned a card in, received a call from a Campus Crusade worker, and agreed with enthusiasm to meet him in the student union. Ron said,

> He shared the plan of salvation with me and then asked if I wanted to make a personal decision for Christ. At the time I said no, and he didn't pressure me. But I took the booklet home and read it over and over. Shortly after that I prayed to receive Christ.

Josh McDowell, who has traveled all over the States speaking to university crowds, says:

> The university is where I came to Christ. I love the give and take of the university world. Often more people there are willing to consider truth than in any other segment of society.[7]

In the university there is a particular group of students with whom we believers should be more involved, the international students. These students are often open to the Lord, both because they are young and because they are lonely here in a foreign land. Often they are also the future leaders of their countries. Steve and I have grown to respect an organization called International Students, Inc.[8] This Christian group has a staff active in many colleges and universities. The following excerpt is from their newspaper:

> We talk about going to the mission field, but fail to notice the mission field here. In fact, the frontiers of foreign missions are in our neighborhoods and on our campuses. One Christian in America could be instrumental in reaching an entire nation for Christ by influencing a key individual from such a country. Though that country might be closed to American missionaries, it can be evangelized by reaching just one of its citizens residing here.
>
> The greatest evangelist China has ever known, John Sung, came to the Lord while a student in the United States. He's called "the father of 10,000 churches." He preached to millions of people throughout China during the communist takeover in the late 1940's.
>
> One of the greatest church planters in India, Bakht Singh, was converted to Christ and discipled while a student in North America. There are many others like him.[9]

If you write to International Students, they'll be happy to put you on their mailing list and give you specific ideas for action. Pat Kershaw, who is on their staff, gives the following ideas:

> You can be a "host" family to an international. Call your local campus office and volunteer to be a home away from home for a

student from a foreign land. Invite him over for supper. Take him shopping and show him your favorite discount store or ice cream shop. Encourage him to stop in for tea whenever he'd like a visit.

When we lived in Fargo we were the host family for two Iranian sisters. These gracious women added so much to our lives and the lives of our children that year. Christmas Eve shared with them was one of the most memorable we've ever had. We talked about the troubles America and Iran were having that year—how they felt, how we felt. We sang carols in front of the fire. We gave them flannel nightgowns (in response to their comments about North Dakota winters) and they gave the children a vocabulary game and then proceeded to beat them soundly in the next rollicking hour!

Now I have a much stronger conviction about the importance of supporting groups like Young Life, Youth for Christ, International Students, Inc., Navigators, Inter-Varsity Christian Fellowship, and Campus Crusade with prayer, money, and volunteer labor. They are working with groups ripe for harvesting.

People in crisis. People who are going through a traumatic time in their lives are part of the fertile field. I've already talked about the importance of being alert for people like this who are part of your daily life. Another way to become involved with people in crisis is by finding a ministry that offers support to hurting people.

When Brennt and Sharon moved to a new city, they prayed for a specific ministry. Brennt had a demanding job and they were also the parents of two toddlers, so their time was limited. But, as Brennt explained,

> There are so many needs in this world. Obviously we can't do it all. But Sharon and I looked for one specific workable thing we could do. Sharon's a great cook and we have a large old home with an extra bedroom. So we decided to put our name on a list at the local hospital as a free place for an out-of-town relative to stay while a loved one is hospitalized.

That ministry has been fruitful. One woman who lost her baby, and then had to have tests herself at the hospital, was a guest in Sharon and Brennt's home. This woman was in great need of the love of Christ—and she found it in Sharon and Brennt. They cared about her, prayed for her, listened to her, drove her to the hospital. Eventually they saw her place her trust in Jesus. Their love, demonstrated in a tangible way, drew her to the Lord.

Many groups work specifically with people in crisis, and Christians should be among those filling their volunteer and paid positions. Youth centers, homes for unwed mothers, drug and rehabilitation programs, nursing homes, hospitals, Big Brother Programs—these are just a few examples of places where it is possible to minister to people in need. Some of these organizations already have Bible studies or support groups, but they could use more Christian staff workers.

When Jesus is lovingly lifted up to people in crisis, some are likely to respond. Debra, for example, told me:

> I was severely depressed, suicidal, after the end of a five-year relationship which had been my source of happiness. I turned to drugs and alcohol to fill that emptiness. Then I was really in trouble and I didn't know which way to turn. . . . It was at a Bible study at the Washington Drug Rehabilitation Center that I came to realize that I could have a relationship with Jesus Christ.

Debra overcame her drug addiction through the power of Christ. He filled her loneliness and gave her a reason for living.

Charlie is a narcotics investigator. When I asked him if he had opportunities to share Christ with the other men on his staff, he told me he had many more opportunities with the men whom he arrested. The men in crisis were more open to help. He shook his head in amazement as he told me:

> I mean, I'm the one who is responsible for sending them to prison, and yet many of them are really open to listening to me. I talk to them about what a mess they are in. I tell them it's time to take stock of their lives and consider the only one who can really help them: Jesus Christ. And they listen to me. They want to hear more.

Charlie has seen Christ turn criminals into new persons.

Steve and I have another friend who chose to specialize in surgical oncology (cancer surgery) because those patients are so needy and open to spiritual guidance.

We know the One who can reconcile men and women to God and who can give them power to live transformed lives. Shouldn't we all, then, be making choices that will increase our contact with men and women in need?

If you are facing a career decision, I'd like to suggest getting in touch with InterCristo.[10] This organization matches Christians with worldwide job opportunities. You'll be asked to fill out a form indicating your interests and skills. They in turn will provide you with information on suitable openings. It's possible the Lord will work through InterCristo to help you find a job where you are really needed.

Try This:
● Are there children in your neighborhood who don't go to Sunday school? Call and ask their parents if you may pick them up and take them with you.

6
Satan's Schemes: Some Ways Christians Blow It

*As long as we seek to impress others that we are right
and they are wrong, we will merely drive them away.*
—Em Griffin[1]

*We must struggle to listen through their ears
and look through their eyes so as to grasp what prevents
them from hearing the gospel and seeing Christ . . .*
—John Stott[2]

SATAN OUR ENEMY desperately wants to keep us from being effective for Christ. He wants us to blow it with non-Christians so they are turned off before they hear our message. Sometimes we settle for superficial relationships with others, and things that matter just don't come up between us. Or we may fail to listen carefully enough. We may talk too much. We may get impatient and angry if we encounter resistance to our words. Let's look at these problem areas and see how we can improve.

Superficial Relationships
One of Satan's main schemes is to keep our relationships with non-Christians superficial. He knows that the closer we get, the greater the danger he will lose one of his captives. So, as we're developing a friendship, Satan whispers: "If you're going to win the world for Christ, you'd better not dally too long with this

insignificant person. He'll probably never be interested in spiritual things anyhow. Move along to someone else. Hurry up." That argument can sound convincing. When it comes to mind we need to stop, recognize our enemy, and bring out our rebuttal.

Genuine friendships take time. If you hurry, there's no way you can have anything but a superficial relationship. And superficial relationships don't bear the kind of fruit that deep relationships bear. Why? Let's look at a few of the reasons.

Friendship increases tolerance. If a person cares about you and knows you care about him, he'll put up with you even though your words may make him uncomfortable. Talking about Jesus and His claims on our lives is a weighty subject. Not only is it difficult for a non-Christian to comprehend, it's difficult to hear.

Some of the people I interviewed told me they were uneasy when the subject of personal faith was initiated. When the talk turned to sin, repentance, and their need for a Savior, many of them felt like leaving the scene. "Why didn't you?" I asked. Almost invariably they would tell me they didn't want to be rude to their friend. Here are some examples of how friendship increased tolerance:

> One day my business partner came in, placed a Christian book on the counter, and said: "Here's a book you might like to read." I looked at the book and felt no interest—but because I cared about my relationship with Bob I decided to go through the form of showing interest by reading the book. Through that book, I, my wife, our whole family came to put our trust in Christ.

> Once, after we had had a particularly good time together, Larry asked if he could come over some night that week and share some things about Jesus with us. We liked Larry and we didn't want to hurt his feelings, so we agreed. Later, Larry invited us to his church. Because we wanted to please him, we went.

Tolerance is also a valuable factor if the gospel is new to your listener. Warfield Munce, a missionary to Japan, told me that because the Japanese have so little exposure to Christianity, some of its ideas are difficult for them to grasp. Therefore, if they don't know you well, they will simply tune you out. So Warfield concentrates on developing relationships. After he strikes up an acquaintance with a Japanese man, he'll suggest having lunch together. He spends time getting to know the individual. That way, when Warfield feels led to bring up the subject of Jesus Christ, he doesn't get tuned out. He explained, "Because my friend has a relationship with me, for the sake of that relationship, he will try to understand what I am saying."

Friendship increases credibility. Another reason Satan wants us to keep our relationships with non-Christians superficial is that he knows if they're with us too much they'll be able to see firsthand the difference Jesus is making in our lives.

Jesus makes a difference. Though you may be very aware of your sinfulness and of the times you fail the Lord, still, Jesus is making a difference in your life. Your unsaved friend will see that difference if he or she has a chance to spend time with you.

Is credibility important? You bet it is. It is more important than ever in this era when advertising campaigns bombard our homes. People have become skeptical and resistant. Everyone, from toothpaste manufacturers to politicians to born-again Christians, is making grandiose claims about what something or someone can do for your life. Who is to be believed?

The people I interviewed were frequently drawn to a person's message after being with her or him for a while. Listen to these comments:

> Jim had been rowdy and rebellious—he ran away from home once as a teenager. When he rededicated his life he did a complete about-face. His unwavering commitment got me thinking more than any other thing.

> The atmosphere in my girlfriend's home was so different from mine. My parents were always arguing; I didn't even want to be at home. But Beth's dad was always all smiles and her mother was just great. The whole family would sit around for an hour after supper—everyone reluctant to leave the conversation and warmth.

Of course we need to be living committed lives. Christ must be making a difference. We need to be walking close to Him and asking Him to cleanse us whenever we sin and letting Him abide in us so that our lives will be filled with His Spirit and His joy. David expressed it this way:

> "Create in me a pure heart, O God,
> and renew a steadfast spirit within me.
> Do not cast me from your presence
> or take your Holy Spirit from me.
> Restore to me the joy of your salvation
> and grant me a willing spirit, to sustain me.
> Then I will teach transgressors your ways,
> and sinners will turn back to you."
> (Psalm 51:10-13)

David is saying that when our hearts are right with God, our lives will reflect that. We will have a credibility that causes others to consider the reality of God. Yet Satan tries to discourage us, and we often wonder if the time we are spending with an individual is going to mean anything in the long run.

It is important therefore, to pray about whom to befriend. Give priority to the fertile field. Be alert to those to whom the Lord alerts you. Then be patient. Don't let Satan discourage you. He'll try; he knows the deeper the friendship, the greater the chances he'll lose one of his captives.

The following mental exercise might help you the next time Satan tells you you're spending too much time with one person. Imagine you had an unsaved brother living a thousand miles away. Wouldn't you be glad to hear that he had become good friends with a Christian? Wouldn't it give you hope that because of that friendship your brother might finally understand the gospel? If that is what we hope and pray for our loved ones, doesn't it make sense that we too should be willing to become good friends with particular non-Christians in our lives?

To become good friends with unbelievers, however, we must equip ourselves for battle. To do that, one verse should be emblazoned in our minds:

"My dear brothers, take note of this: Everyone should be quick to listen, slow to speak and slow to become angry, for man's anger does not bring about the righteous life that God desires" (James 1:19-20).

Are You Quick to Listen?

Good listeners are as rare as buffalo nickels. I remember a conversation I had with a friend in a little restaurant on an island in Washington State. As soon as she discovered I was a born-again Christian, she proceeded to tell me about her Uncle Gerald.

> At every family gathering Uncle Gerald tells us about all the wonderful things the Lord is doing through him and his family. Their family never has any of the troubles that plague our side: no rebellious children, no divorce, no financial worries... He monopolizes the conversation and nobody can get a word in edgewise. And every ⌐hristmas we can count on getting a lengthy form letter from Uncle Gerald listing his triumphs. There's never one question asking about our lives. Not even a simple "How are you?"

As my friend was describing her Uncle Gerald I felt embarrassed and ashamed. Is that how we Christians seem to the world? Do we go on and on about our triumphs, never listening, never caring? Christians should be the best listeners of all. Though I don't think most of us are as bad as Uncle Gerald, still, listening is an art we've failed to develop.

A good listener isn't simply someone who is quiet (though that helps), but someone who knows how to be "the host in conversation," as Rebecca Pippert has put it. With a caring heart, a good listener is able to ask questions and respond in a way that will draw another person out. Proverbs 20:5 says: "The purposes of a man's heart are deep waters, but a man of understanding draws them out."

We can't expect to understand people before we listen to them. John Stott stresses the importance of having a "steadfast resolve to rid our minds of the prejudices and caricatures which we may entertain" about non-Christians.[3] We can't expect people to believe a certain way simply because they belong to a certain denomination. People defy the stereotypes. And we can't expect all the unchurched to be the same either. All persons are different, with a unique heritage and set of experiences which make them react as they do to Christ and His followers. That's why we must have genuine dialogue with non-Christian friends and try to understand. John Stott says we must

> Struggle to listen through their ears and look through their eyes so as to grasp what prevents them from hearing the gospel and seeing Christ; to sympathize with them in all of their doubts, fears, and hangups.[4]

Empathy. Perhaps the best way to draw a person out is by finding points of identification. What do you have in common? I've often thought about Paul's method as he explained it in 1 Corinthians:

> "Though I am free and belong to no man, I make myself a slave to everyone, to win as many as possible. To the Jews I became like a Jew, to win the Jews. . . . To the weak I became weak, to win the weak. I have become all things to all men so that by all possible means I might save some" (1 Cor. 9:19, 22).

When your friend is answering one of your questions, listen and look for points of identification. James Engel says it is best to

> start with genuine empathy for other persons, even if they are wrong in what they believe. Be content to identify with them where they are and move from there patiently, realizing that change is often slow.[5]

Many of the people whom you and I are likely to befriend consider themselves Christians. They would be deeply offended by an approach that assumed they were not. Some of these people genuinely may be Christians; others simply may not understand what it really means, scripturally, to be a Christian. In either case, it is best to approach a person like this with empathy. Treat him or her as if they are a Christian and will therefore be interested in spiritual things.

When Lynn discovered that Judy went to church, she shared things she'd been learning from the Word and sometimes asked Judy for her opinion. Judy said:

> This was all new to me but I decided not to let Lynn know that. I wasn't sure I believed all the things she did, but then again, I wasn't sure I didn't.

Judy came to have a vital relationship with Christ, in part, I believe, because of the gentle way she was approached.

Satan encourages us to draw battle lines, to rush in without listening. If we approach someone as an "unbeliever," that person will begin to act like an unbeliever and think up reasons for not believing. How much better to treat them as if they would be interested. If you don't paint them as a heathen, but instead empathize with their spiritual perceptions, you will be opening a door and encouraging dialogue. Empathize, listen, and listen some more.

Are You Slow to Speak?

Some Christians feel they are witnessing when they comment negatively on some undesirable habit. That isn't witnessing, it's erecting barriers. Our message is Christ, not, "stop swearing, stop smoking, stop listening to rock music." When we lift up Christ in His holiness, people will see themselves as they are without our having to drum it in. But if we start with peripheral things, that is, the habits that we (and maybe God) find offensive, we may cause that person to become defensive and never hear the gospel. Be slow to speak about what offends you—remember that your main goal is to love the person into the Kingdom.

I enjoyed interviewing Marilyn, a Christian who has opened her home to young people in need. Marilyn told me that more than thirty years ago, before her conversion, she spent her spring break in Seattle with her Aunt Jo. The college dance was coming and Marilyn decided to ask Aunt Jo to take her shopping for a dress.

Aunt Jo was a Christian who had some strong convictions about the evils of dancing. When Marilyn told her what she wanted, Aunt Jo could have refused and given her a sermon about dances. Instead, Aunt Jo held her tongue. She even took Marilyn shopping. Why? Because she was praying and hoping to present Christ to her niece during that vacation, and she didn't want to stumble on a peripheral issue. A wise woman.

When Aunt Jo invited Marilyn to church, Marilyn went but didn't particularly like it. She explained:

> I thought the pastor was really quite noisy. He preached the gospel and made me uncomfortable. That night Aunt Jo asked me if I'd like to go again, but I said, "No, I don't think so. I think I'll wash my hair." Aunt Jo didn't pressure me. When I found I was out of shampoo I agreed to walk with her on her way to church and just go as far as the drugstore for shampoo and then come back. The drugstore was closed. Then Aunt Jo mentioned that instead of the regular pastor three young fellows would be giving their testimony. That sounded more interesting so I agreed to go.

At that service those testimonies stirred Marilyn's heart. At the invitation she raised her hand. Marilyn, her Aunt Jo, and the pastor went into his office and talked about Jesus and Marilyn's need to respond to Him. She became a Christian that night.

Later as Marilyn lay in her bed, she wondered if she had really been forgiven, if she was really a child of God. Then she heard her Aunt singing, "There's a new name written down in glory, and it's Marilyn's, yes, it's Marilyn's . . ." Marilyn thought, "Well, if Aunt Jo says it's true, it must be so."

For ten years Emmy-Lou and Clayton prayed for their neighbor, Bruce. Bruce was into several activities his Christian neighbors could have confronted him about, but chose not to. Bruce had raised $100,000 for the city through the promotion of gambling. Emmy-Lou and Clayton didn't talk about the morality of gambling. Bruce was a heavy smoker, so when he came over, Emmy-Lou provided ash trays. An alcoholic, Bruce spent most evenings at his men's club. Again, though they knew

Jesus could deliver him, they chose not to attack his drinking. As Emmy-Lou said,

> Had we tried to talk to Bruce about any of those things, he never would have given them up. But after he came to the Lord, one by one, he gave them all up.

What did Emmy-Lou and Clayton talk to Bruce about? Jesus. They explained who Jesus was and why He came, and they were silent about side issues. Bruce told me Clayton would sometimes go with him to his men's club:

> That couldn't have been too comfortable a situation for Clayton— basically a bunch of guys sitting around drinking. But he came, ordered a soft drink, and listened to me. Now I realize what an act of love that was.

When I interviewed Bruce he had several stacks of Christian books piled on the floor around his easy chair (his new haunt is the Christian book store). He has an insatiable thirst for the Word. My heart was warmed as this gray-headed man told me of the transformation in his life. Jesus had taken care of the peripheral issues. Emmy-Lou and Clayton didn't have to say a word about them.

What if our friend initiates a discussion on a peripheral issue? If so, we need to discern whether it's a red herring or a genuine concern. When Billy Graham appeared on a Phil Donahue show broadcast from Las Vegas, he was explaining the gospel when Donahue cut in and asked, "Is it all right for a Christian to gamble?" Dr. Graham was courteous, but took the conversation right back to the central issue: "We have great freedom in Christ, but the greatest gamble a man takes is the gamble for his soul."

If our friend sincerely wants to know our thoughts on a peripheral issue, he'll persist. If the issue is clear-cut in Scripture, then we must say so. We have to present an honest picture of the lordship of Christ.

One time, after I had shared the gospel with a young woman,

she was silent for a minute and then looked at me with tears in her eyes: "You don't know just how much I would like to have Jesus in my life, Dee. But I'm afraid He would tell me to give Tom up" (Tom was her married boyfriend). I had to agree with her. Scripture is clear about the immorality of adultery. I did tell her that although I knew it would be hard, I also knew that God's ways are always best. He didn't give the commandment on adultery to hurt her, but because He loved her and He knew what was best for her.

One habit that non-Christians bring up fairly regularly is drinking. As one friend said to me, "My husband and I like to drink. If we got into this (commitment to Christ), would we have to stop drinking?" Her question was straightforward and sincere. It was no red herring. She wanted to know.

I've struggled with how to answer because I don't want to reduce Christianity to teetotaling. In many parts of the world, Christians regularly drink wine. I also know that Scripture calls for moderation in this regard, not for abstinence.

On the other hand, my husband, who treats patient after patient with alcohol-related problems, is an abstainer on the basis of "right reason." Medical textbooks show that more than 50 percent of abusing families,[6] more than 50 percent of traffic fatalities,[7] and more than 33 percent of suicides are directly related to drinking.[8] Seven percent of Americans have alcohol-related problems.[9] Steve says he would never board an airplane that had a 7 percent chance of having an accident! "Even if a Christian is confident he can limit his own drinking to moderation," Steve says, "he can never be sure that his children and others watching his example will be able to do that."

It's a complex issue, but perhaps the best response is one that Ann gave George when he was continually bringing up the issue of drinking at a beginners' Bible study. She said, "If your drinking is a problem, George, the Lord will convict you of it. I don't think we'll get anywhere trying to hash it out before then." (George's drinking was a problem and, with the Spirit's power, he gave it up a year later.)

When my sister Sally presented the gospel to me I remember telling her that Steve and I had always planned to build a luxurious home on the Pacific Ocean. "If I gave my life to Jesus," I asked, "would I have to give that up?" Sensing that I had a problem similar to the rich young ruler's, Sally told me that, in my case, she thought the house would have to go. She said that Jesus said,

> "For whoever wants to save his life will lose it, but whoever loses his life for me and for the gospel will save it. What good is it for a man to gain the whole world, yet forfeit his soul?" (Mark 8:35-36).

The story of the rich young ruler (Luke 18:18-27) may be a good one to tell if your friend asks you, "Am I going to have to give up such and such?" Then that individual can decide if this is something she or he has put before God. In my case, I'm thankful that Sally asked me to count the cost. It challenged me and made me realize what an important decision I faced. But I'm also glad Sally didn't start with the cost, but rather with Jesus Himself.

The lesson? Be slow to speak on tangential issues. Our central message is Jesus.

Are You Slow to Become Angry?

The subject of Jesus and a person's response to Him is the most important subject we'll ever discuss. So, understandably, emotions run high. But it pays to remember that we cannot argue anyone into the kingdom of heaven. A quarrel may actually harden the other person's heart. If we argue with people, they are going to defend themselves. Em Griffin of Wheaton College gives a sober warning that "the more a person thinks up reasons for not believing, the more he becomes immune to even a winsome presentation of the gospel."[10] The apostle Paul wrote,

> "The Lord's servant must not quarrel; instead he must be kind to everyone, able to teach, not resentful. Those who oppose him he must gently instruct, in the hope that God will grant them repentance leading them to a knowledge of the truth, and that they will

come to their senses and escape from the trap of the devil, who has taken them captive to do his will" (2 Tim. 2:24-26).

The way to react to opposition, Paul says, is with gentle instruction. We shouldn't resent non-believers; it is the devil who is blinding them and has them captive. Even in North America many have never heard a clear presentation of the gospel. Many have never had the advantages of a Christian home or a Christ-centered church. So approach others gently, in hope and with prayer that God will lead them to a knowledge of the truth.

Deb belonged to a youth group in a large liberal church in Nebraska. The group was so rowdy, their teachers kept quitting. Carol, a young public school teacher, had been praying for an opportunity to work with a high school youth group. She heard about the group in Deb's church and volunteered for the position. The group soon began meeting in Carol's home on Monday nights.

The first Monday, Carol gave her testimony and presented the gospel. During the entire presentation, the kids snickered and laughed. Carol didn't think they'd ever be back.

But the next Monday they all came back bringing a few additional friends. They played games and then, once again, Carol presented the gospel. The kids giggled through the whole talk and Carol cried after they left. But she was so burdened for them that, despite her anger and hurt, she was determined to continue sharing her faith as long as they kept coming back.

Seven weeks and seven presentations of the gospel later, Carol asked the group if they were getting anything out of her talks. One teen said that he had made a commitment to Christ. Then Deb indicated that she had too. Several other hands went up showing group members who had become Christians.

I later asked Deb why they all gave Carol such a hard time. "Maybe it was peer pressure," Deb said. "We didn't want the others to know we were taking her seriously, but many of us were. I know I would go home and think hard about the things Carol had said."

Carol's burden for the group kept her from showing her hurt and anger, and the kids responded to her love and faithfulness.

Sometimes, despite a gentle presentation of the gospel, our friends will react to us with hostility or rejection. If they reject Christ and His claims on their life, they may reject us too. It may become difficult for them to be around us. As Paul explained,

> "For we are to God the aroma of Christ among those who are being saved and those who are perishing. To the one we are the smell of death; to the other, the fragrance of life" (2 Cor. 2:15-16).

Who wants to be around someone who is "the smell of death"? It hurts when a friend rejects you, but if you are sure it is because he is rejecting Christ Himself, and not because you have been insensitive, you must graciously accept that rejection. That is bound to happen at times in your life if you are consistently sharing the gospel. Jesus said to keep in mind that if we are hated by the world, it hated Him first (John 15:18). Accept this rejection in a spirit of love and take comfort in Jesus' promise:

> "Blessed are you when people insult you, persecute you and falsely say all kinds of evil against you because of me. Rejoice and be glad, because great is your reward in heaven" (Matt. 5:11-12a).

Love people into the kingdom. Don't respond to anger with anger. The way to win others is with love. If people know we love them, they are much more responsive. Listen to these comments from my interviews:

> This stout little pastor would climb three flights of stairs to visit us in our hot apartment that summer in Evanston. He'd wipe his brow with a handkerchief and graciously accept a glass of water. He simply visited with us, showing us we were important to him.

> I was uneasy at church because I felt so inferior. I didn't know the Bible at all and my life simply didn't measure up. But these people just loved me and accepted me as one of them. Their love cast out all my fear.

Gordon and Ray treated me like a brother from the start. They showed me gently what light was. They loved me in.

A Lesson in Cultural Sensitivity

Finally, I want to address an important issue relating to sensitivity to others. The example concerns a large segment of our population: feminists. Some of my friends thought I would be wise to delete this section of the book altogether, afraid it might offend some readers who would then dismiss the rest of what I say. I pray this will not be—but if you disagree with the idea of even discussing this topic, I ask you to lovingly overlook my attempt to do so, skip this part, and go on to the rest of the book.

By *feminist* I'm referring not only to women who worked and marched for the ERA. I'm thinking about *every* person who has been in sympathy with parts of the women's liberation movement.[11] That includes almost everyone, I believe, but in particular the forty-two million American women who are holding jobs outside the home.[12]

During the early years of the feminist movement, a rift developed between many feminists and evangelicals. Feminist leaders were taking, perhaps of necessity, a strong stand—and many evangelicals perceived that stand, perhaps justifiably, as a threat to the home. The problem is that, instead of being quick to hear, slow to speak, and slow to become angry, many Christians reacted violently and that rift has continued. Now, when we'd like to get secular feminists to hear the gospel of Christ, we can't get them to come close enough to listen. The time has come for us to take the initiative in mending fences with feminists.

How Secular Feminists Perceive Christians. Communication experts tell us that, when considering the effect of a message, the important point is not what you or I intended to convey, but what is actually perceived. For several reasons, many secular feminists perceive that "born-again Christians" have a doctrine about women that goes something like this:

1. Women were created for the sole purpose of helping men.
   A. Women are inferior to men.
   B. Women are best suited for supportive positions.
   C. Single women are outcasts.
2. It is un-Christian and unscriptural to believe in equality between the sexes.

How did feminists develop that perception of Christianity? To understand, it helps to look at some history.

The 1970s and "Total Women." In the sixties and early seventies, the contemporary feminist movement arose and mushroomed. Betty Friedan's *The Feminine Mystique* is often credited with opening millions of women's eyes. I believe that many of Friedan's observations were just and necessary. Women did not receive equal pay for equal work. (Even in 1982, salaried women in the U.S. earned only fifty-seven cents for every dollar earned by men. The proportion of women to men in managerial positions remained slim.)

The problem was much deeper, however, than equal pay for equal work, or even equal opportunity. Feminists felt that there was an ingrained cultural attitude that women were less important than men, that they were best suited to inferior positions. They felt that women's worth as persons was being disregarded, their talents not being used. As women returned to salaried work in astonishing numbers, they wanted to be treated fairly. They wanted their pleas to be heard. They were being discriminated against.

It's characteristic of any revolution to be extreme in the beginning, and some feminist leaders gave the impression that men were the enemy. That extreme position did threaten marriage and the home. In reaction to it came a flood of Christian books that exalted men and told women their only hope of fulfillment was in complete, unquestioning submission to men. One woman told what happened in her small study group, in 1971, when *Fascinating Womanhood* took her church by storm:

Our fellowship had begun as a Bible study for Christians searching for a New Testament faith. After *Fascinating Womanhood,* it was only natural to take all the Scriptures regarding women in the most literal sense. Some of the women began wearing head-covers to indicate their submissiveness. We were instructed to stifle deliberately the gifts of the Holy Spirit which we had always practiced in church, so that our husbands would be forced to take a more active role. It was constantly emphasized how important the leadership of men was—since Eve had been deceived, our sex was forever unfit for any kind of decision-making or administration.

A friend of mine had a very difficult childbirth with complications. That, she was told, was God's punishment for having been unsubmissive. When her husband recommended she have a tubal ligation, she felt she dare not disagree. Though tears streamed down her face all the way to the hospital, the operation was performed. Later, she fell into a deep depression and lost all sexual feelings. When she spoke to the pastor about these problems, he advised her to "fake it."[13]

In 1973 Marabel Morgan's *Total Woman* appeared. Through this book and related seminars, women were taught to view their men as their "kings" and to cater to their special quirks "whether it be in salads, sex, or sports!"[14] Marabel Morgan's basic premise was that "It is only when a woman surrenders her life to her husband, reveres and worships him, and is willing to serve him, that she becomes really beautiful to him."[15] The Bible was quoted for support. Three million copies of the hardcover edition were sold in the first three years and virtually every TV talk show gave the author publicity. Soon she had a bestselling paperback and a sequel, *Total Joy,* which made the cover of *Time* in 1977. The *New York Times Magazine* called her views a "counterrevolution" and the cover featured a woman dressed in a scanty black pirate outfit ready to meet and "inspire" her husband after a long day's work.

Letters to the editors of secular magazines were filled with rage. *Time's* senior editor found that the mere mention of Marabel Morgan's name at a Long Island dinner party brought

a hostile response from the women present.[16] One writer specu-
lated that the major reason "for the hostility to Marabel Morgan
is the belief that she preaches a return to days of unfairness and
unequality."[17]

To be truthful, my initial reaction to *The Total Woman* was
positive. At a time when feminist leaders were screaming "me-
first," Marabel's specific assignments to be loving were refreshing. In 1973 Steve was in the middle of his residency in
Akron. Like many of my friends in the same situation, I was
weary of my husband's long hours away and of being totally
responsible for our children. A few residents' wives believed the
feminists' promise that there was a better life waiting if they
could be free of their man. Some were murmuring of mutiny.
I knew I didn't want mutiny and *The Total Woman* seemed like
a more positive alternative. My friend Lee and I had a coffee for
other residents' wives to come and discuss *The Total Woman.*
Their hostile reaction that day should have warned me to listen
to them, but I didn't. They didn't think Marabel's book was
funny or helpful—they thought it was a travesty of justice.

After *Total Woman,* feminists became aware of other Christian books on marriage. The following excerpt is from an article
in *Ms.:*

> A submissive nature is the miracle for which religious women pray.
> No one has prayed harder, longer, and with less apparent success
> than Anita Bryant. She has spent a good part of her life on her
> knees begging Jesus to forgive her for the sin of existing... She
> did not want to marry. In particular, she did not want to marry Bob
> Green. He 'won' her through a war of attrition. Every 'No' on her
> part was taken as a 'Yes' by him. He hounded her. Having got his
> hooks into her, especially knowing how to hit on her rawest nerve,
> guilt over the abnormality of her ambition, by definition unwomanly
> and potentially satanic, Green has manipulated Bryant in a manner
> nearly unmatched in modern love stories. One begins to see a
> woman hemmed in, desperately trying to please a husband who
> manipulates and harasses her and whose control of her life on every
> level is virtually absolute.[18]

Could it be that there was some truth, albeit exaggerated, in the feminist perceptions? Could it be that, in reaction to extreme statements by some feminists, we evangelicals went beyond Scripture, and that was having an unhealthy effect on our marriages?

In addition to failing to be "swift to hear," we failed to be "slow to speak and slow to become angry." Unkind words flew. Here are statements from letters published in a national Christian magazine in 1975:

> I see feminism as a threat to Christianity and a tool of Satan.

> The feminist movement is bent on destroying the home, motherhood, and family. And yes, we should stand against it as unscriptural and unChristian.

> A nationwide revival would take care of the feminist movement.[19]

The '70s decade is over. Have emotions simmered down? Perhaps we are coming back to some middle position. I see now that many Christian books on marriage were a polarized reaction to feminism, not a true picture of the Scriptures. I believe my husband is the head of our home, but he is not my king (my king is Jesus) and together, as joint-heirs, we seek the will of God for our daily lives. Because we are both sinful we need each other's wisdom and exhortation to find and stay on the right path.

I feel sad about our reaction to feminism in the past decade. When people are suffering, you should listen to them intently and try to find points of empathy. Even if you don't agree about everything, there should at least be an honest attempt to see others' perspectives and care about their pain. That is true no matter what the issue.

What Now?
Evangelical Christianity has blundered with a phenomenal number of women, millions, but I am hopeful that the breach can be mended. I have some specific suggestions.

First, it could be helpful to read some material sympathetic to feminist concerns. There will be points with which you'll disagree, but look for points of empathy. Isn't that what Paul meant when he said he wanted to "become all things to all men so that if possible he might save some" (1 Cor. 9:22)?

Second, when you have an opportunity to talk to a woman who has chosen to take a job outside the home, be careful not to create a rift over this peripheral issue. Our goal is to make friends with non-Christians and love them into the kingdom. It's not going to help if we say in a "holier than thou" tone, "I feel it's *my* responsibility to be a full-time mother to my children."

On the other hand, if you happen to be an evangelical feminist, you may need to look for points of identification with those who don't share your viewpoint. Don't assume without listening that they have nothing to say to you. Proverbs 18:13 says "He who answers before listening—that is his folly and his shame."

Try This:

● Is your life the kind that would draw failing, fearful people to the Savior? Find a Christian friend with whom you can be completely honest. Confess your sins to that person and ask him or her to pray for you.

● Start a list of questions you'd like to ask a friend the next time you get together. Post the list in a visible place and jot down more questions as they come to mind.

● Buy a large ash tray and put it in your living room. Even if no one ever uses it, it can be a reminder to you that you won't destroy the work of God over a cigarette.

● Think of some specific ways others have made you feel loved. For example, people have brought me homemade pies and casseroles. They've sewn dresses for our daughter and played basketball with our sons. They've dropped in on me because they missed me. They've hugged me and told me I'm special. Write down *your* list and work on showing that kind of love this week.

● An evangelical feminist I have come to respect, because of her thorough approach to Scripture and her conviction that it is the literal word of God, is Patricia Gundry. Read one of her books: *Woman, Be Free* or *Heirs Together.*

7
A Life with a Message

Our problem in evangelism is not that we don't have enough information—it is that we don't know how to be ourselves...
—Rebecca Manley Pippert[1]

I heard the gospel at a Christian Women's Club luncheon. I thought, "I've been in church all my life but I never understood I needed a personal relationship with Jesus."
—a woman from Council Bluffs, Iowa

JOE BAYLY HAS WRYLY COMMENTED that Christian coffee never saved anyone. It's true—in addition to being loved, women and men must hear the message of Christ. Perhaps they will hear it when we invite them to a Bible study or to a talk by a Christian speaker (more about that later). But in most cases people hear on a one-to-one basis.

I don't want to give the impression that you should nurture a friendship for several months, keep your faith under cover, and then suddenly shift and let your friend see your spiritual side. At the very start of a friendship, if you are yourself, you will quite naturally comment from time to time about spiritual things.

The Struggle to Be Authentic and Guileless
In *Evangelism as a Lifestyle,* Jim Petersen says:

> It has been my experience that I need to talk about my faith early in a relationship. I've found the longer I wait, the more difficult it becomes. Patterns develop in a friendship that are hard to break out of later. We don't have to say much at the outset; often just enough to "get the flag up" will suffice.[2]

Patterns in a friendship are hard to break. If I haven't been myself from the beginning of a friendship, if I have stifled my spiritual responses during conversation, it is hard to start revealing them a few weeks or months later. True, you don't want to come on so strong that you frighten friends away before you get to know them. But neither should there be a cloud of spiritual silence hanging over you.

Here are some comments that people remembered being made at the start of a friendship:

> Barb asked me about our church. Being new in town, they were looking for one to attend. She asked me if we studied the Bible, if there were small groups that met for Bible study and prayer. I didn't think there were and her questions got my mind spinning.

> Karen told me she'd been listening to a series on Christian marriage on the radio station. She said, "I think even we who have good marriages need all the help we can get." I was interested and so the next day she called when it was on and told me where to tune in. I listened to this Pastor Swindoll and then Karen and I had this in common to talk about.

Notice what Barb and Karen had in common. Quite naturally with a new friend they shared thoughts that had been occupying their minds. They assumed interest on the part of their listener. That genuine approach opened the door for future conversations.

If there's a secret in evangelism, it's to be yourself. If you are spending time with the Lord, if you are trying to do His will, an authentic spiritual dimension will be there. Although you don't want to overwhelm your friend, neither should you be continually stifling spiritual comments that naturally arise.

Perhaps one reason new Christians are particularly fruitful is that they are spontaneous. They simply and enthusiastically tell others about what has happened to them. Why is it such a struggle later on for us to be authentic, to approach people without guile? Why is it so difficult to be natural and spontaneous? I can think of two possibilities. First, some of us may be the victims of bad evangelistic training, training that actually encouraged us to be artificial. Second, all of us are a bit hesitant to let others see us as we really are, for fear they'll withdraw. Let's look at those two possibilities.

1. Have you had bad evangelistic training? I remember a sermon by a visiting speaker entitled "Fishing for Men." He compared witnessing to angling. His main points were:

1. Go where the fish are!
2. Prepare your bait.
3. Hide your hook.
4. Tease him, trick him, jerk him up!

Is it any wonder that sensitive Christians are uncomfortable with evangelism? I don't like to be tricked or teased—and I certainly wouldn't like discovering a hidden hook! I don't want to use those kinds of tactics on my friends. I want to be able to say,

> "We have renounced secret and shameful ways; we do not use deception, nor do we distort the word of God" (2 Cor. 4:2a).

> "The appeal we make does not spring from error or impure motives, nor are we trying to trick you" (1 Thess. 2:3).

When Jesus talked about fishing for men He wasn't advising trickery. His analogy was to *net* fishing rather than today's sport of *angling;* there are important differences.

Angling	Net fishing
a sport	a way of life
an individual project	a group project
deceptive	natural

As Arthur McPhee observed, "When we transfer imagery like this to our day, we are at a bit of a disadvantage. We automatically think of angling."[3] I have never fished with a net, but I spent many hours as a child catching perch and bass with a hook and worm dropped in Green Bay. But that's not the way the Lord wants us to reach out to others.

When we use deceit or manipulation, we quench the Spirit. If evangelism means I pretend to be taking an "evangelistic survey" when I'm honestly not doing any such thing, if evangelism means I corner some disinterested person into hearing my testimony, or if evangelism means I think up artificial ways to turn the subject to Jesus, then evangelism is definitely not my gift. If you have been a victim of that kind of teaching, I have liberating news for you. That was never the way Jesus intended us to tell others about Him.

In the past I was confused by a passage in Philippians where Paul stated that though some were preaching Christ out of impure motives, still he rejoiced that Christ was being preached. Did that mean, I wondered, that the end justifies the means? I don't think so. I think it means we can rejoice that, *despite* the fact that some motives and methods in evangelism are impure, people are still hearing the gospel and responding. It does not mean that impure motives and methods are to be our model.

Our motivation for sharing our faith should be love for others and obedience to God. If our motive is otherwise we should confess and turn from it so that we can have the full power of the Spirit. Our method, if you can even call it a method, is to be authentic and guileless. We should approach people by gently and naturally sharing the thoughts we have.

2. Are you hesitant to let others see you as you really are? Is it difficult for you to be yourself with others? Are you hesitant to reveal your inner thoughts? That reluctance on our part can be a stopgate holding back a flood of communication. We could be talking honestly with our friends about things that are on our hearts, about the things that matter.

Rebecca Pippert believes that we struggle to relate to others naturally, humanly, because we are uncomfortable with our humanity. If we were to tell a non-Christian what was really on our mind, that would blow our cover. They would discover that we aren't super saints, that we don't have a doctorate in theology, that we are (here it comes!) mere humans.

Yet the very thing we fear, letting non-Christians know what we are thinking, may be the barrier breaker. For example, if we are fearful that talking about spiritual things will offend our friend, Rebecca Pippert suggests we tell her or him why we are hesitating. She relates the following story.

> I began telling my friend about Jesus and she seemed interested. But as I became more enthusiastic about what it meant to be a Christian, she seemed to withdraw emotionally. Still I kept on talking about Jesus—for want of knowing what else to do. But even though my mouth kept moving, I was very aware that I was turning her off. So there I was, having a private conversation with myself, trying to figure out how to stop, while I could hear myself talking to her about Christ.
>
> Suddenly I realized how ridiculous all this was, so I said, "Look, I feel really bad. I am very excited about who God is and what he's done in my life. But I hate it when people push 'religion' on me. So if I'm coming on too strong will you just tell me?"
>
> She looked at me in disbelief. "I can't believe you just said that," she answered.
>
> "Why?" I asked.
>
> "Well, I never knew Christians were aware that we hate being recipients of a running monolog," she answered. (So much for my evangelistic skill.)
>
> "Listen," I responded, "most Christians I know are very hesitant to share their faith *precisely* because they're afraid they'll offend."
>
> "But as long as you let people know that you're aware of where they're coming from, you can say anything you want!" she responded immediately. "And you just tell Christians I said so."[4]

Rebecca's friend was very honest. Everyone might not have responded to her so openly, and in those cases we need to be sensitive to the Spirit's leading as to whether to proceed. But candor usually begets candor. If a person is revealing his heart to me, at some personal risk, I *love* him for it. Because he is making himself vulnerable, I want to listen. I want to understand. And I am stirred to respond with equal candor.

Are you afraid of being an offensive Christian? A little fear can remind you to be gentle and sensitive to the Spirit. But don't allow that fear to keep you from sharing the message. That's the enemy's plan.

Our Message: Relationship with Jesus

The ways in which the individuals I interviewed heard about Jesus were almost as numerous as the individuals themselves. One man heard when a friend joined him for coffee at McDonald's. His friend drew a diagram on a napkin showing the great gulf separating human beings from God and illustrated how Jesus, on the cross, bridged the gap. One woman heard when she tuned her radio to some Christmas music. Following "O Holy Night," a Christian speaker explained the gospel.

Others began to understand the message after a number of weeks in a beginners' Bible study. One man from Hawaii told me that before his conversion he never saw the light of day; he spent his sunlit hours in bars. He was desperate and lonely, but one night in his motel room he picked up a Gideon Bible and discovered Jesus in the Gospel of John. One woman said she saw the face of Jesus saying, "Sheila, you're on the outskirts." One university professor said that he was enlightened when a friend pointed out: "Al, Christianity is not a philosophy or a way of life. It's a personal relationship with Jesus."

God's Spirit moves in various ways. The *way* in which Jesus was lifted up varied in those instances, but the message was always the same: Jesus, and a person's need for a relationship with Him. Our message is not the church, not the sacraments, not religion, but relationship to Jesus.

People have missed the message. Most of the people I interviewed had grown up in America, had attended church at least occasionally, but had the misconception that Christianity was a philosophy, a set of moral teachings. If someone had asked them, "Are you a Christian?" most would have responded affirmatively. They would have interpreted that question as "Are you a moral person?" or "Do you go to church?" Paul Little suggests a better way to phrase that question: "Have you ever trusted Jesus as your Lord and Savior—or are you still on the way?"[5] That approach gently clarifies that becoming a Christian is not equivalent to subscribing to a set of moral principles but instead is a personal response of trust in Jesus.

How can people have missed the basic gospel message? If you were raised in a Christian home, if day by day your family related to Jesus on a personal basis, if all problems and decisions were brought to Him, if you regularly sang the praises "of Him who died for me"—then you may be incredulous that anyone could have missed that message. But they have.

George Gallup has conducted several polls on America's faith. He found that, on the surface, America is impressively "religious."

> Only about one person in 20 says he has no religious preference; we have one of the highest church attendance records in the world; large majorities attest to a belief in God, and in heaven . . . virtually every home has a Bible.[6]

Evangelicals were shocked during Jimmy Carter's first presidential campaign to hear that the Gallup Poll revealed that one-third of Americans considered themselves "born-again." The wording of the question was: "Would you say that you have been born again, or have had a born-again experience—that is, an identifiable turning point in your life?"[7] Nothing about Jesus was mentioned and therefore people could have thought being born-again meant having their first communion or joining a church.

Gallup was unconvinced too. He said, how can so many be born-again and yet be "spiritually illiterate"? He found a shocking lack of knowledge about the Bible. Three out of four did not connect religion with their judgments of right and wrong.

And how, Gallup pondered, can almost all American people say they believe in God, yet be essentially materialistic?[8] Gallup made another attempt in 1982 to discover how many true Christians there are in the U.S. and gave a more definitive description. His percentage dropped to 12 percent.[9]

I think that when many Americans say they "believe" they mean "give mental assent to the facts." When asked to check answers to questions such as: Do you believe in God? Do you believe in Jesus? Do you believe in Heaven? they check "yes, yes, yes." We use terms like *born-again* and *believe* without defining them clearly. Jesus did not mean mental assent to the facts when he used the term *believe.* The Greek word used most frequently in the Gospel of John is *pisteuo.* It means "to believe, also to be persuaded of, and hence to place confidence in, to trust, signifies, in this sense of the word, reliance upon, not mere credence."[10]

Many people have not grasped that being a Christian goes beyond mere credence to a personal commitment to Jesus. A lot of people could echo this comment:

> When I was confirmed I was asked to repeat a creed. In so far as I understood it, when I said it, I meant it. I agreed with those statements. I was, I thought, a Christian. But was Jesus an integral part of my life? No. Was I committed to Him as the Lord of my everyday life? No. Did I actually understand what His crucifixion and resurrection had to do with reconciling me to God? No. Was I saved? I doubt it.

Why are people so in the dark about the central message of the Bible? Why don't people understand that they have to repent of their sins and trust in Christ? Why don't people know that a Christian is someone who is personally related to Jesus as Savior and Lord? It is true that many ministers, who may or may not be born again, have led people astray by not stressing the central issue of relationship to Jesus Christ. At the Lausanne Congress on Evangelism, Tom Rees said:

It is tragically possible to preach the Church instead of Christ, the sacraments instead of the Savior, the creed instead of the Christ, the Scriptures instead of the Son of God.[11]

But we cannot put all the blame on the clergy. Too often we lay Christians think we are sharing the message when we mention that we go to Bible study, we don't drink, or we are opposed, on scriptural grounds, to abortion. These things can be a testimony, but they are not communicating the central message. We must show our friends who Jesus is, why He came to earth, and how a person can respond to Him.

In the early church the believers knew their message:

"Day after day, in the temple courts and from house to house, they never stopped teaching and proclaiming the good news that Jesus is the Christ" (Acts 5:42).

They prayed they would "proclaim it clearly" (Col. 4:4). We must proclaim it clearly too. The need is greater than ever; the waters have been so muddied.

Try This:
- Sometimes I think we don't even know how to be ourselves with other Christians. Spend twenty minutes talking to a close Christian friend or relative today. Practice talking about the spiritual thoughts that have been on your mind lately.
- Define the following terms as simply and clearly as you can. Don't use "scriptural" terminology.
  a. Sin
  b. Repent
  c. Believe
  d. Atonement
  e. Born again
  f. Invite Jesus into your heart

8

Preparing Yourself
to Share
the Gospel

Why don't Christians just tell you what they're thinking?
Why can't they be like my friend in Spokane?
One day she simply said to me: "Sandy, I've had an
experience with Jesus that has changed my life—so I'm
really interested in spiritual things. If you are
at all interested, we can talk. Otherwise, that's fine.
I'll understand."
—Sandy, a young woman from Washington

A FEW OF THE PEOPLE I interviewed seemed to think it was "unspiritual" to prepare their message. Yet we are told to "be prepared to give an answer ... for the hope that we have" (1 Pet. 3:15b). That may take some disciplined hours of preparation. Being prepared certainly doesn't mean we won't be relying on the Spirit's power at the time of presentation. We will be.

The gospel is new to some people, and it can sound like meaningless words and phrases. Scott, an engineering student, said:

> I just couldn't grasp what my friend was saying. He kept telling me "You need to put off the old nature and put on the new." And I would say "Huh?" And he would say "I mean, you need to crucify the flesh and be filled with the Spirit." And I'm still saying "Huh?"

There are two ways to communicate the message of Christ to someone else. You can describe your personal experience of Christ—give your testimony; or you can present the gospel directly. Since those two ways frequently overlap and blend together, it's best to be prepared to do both.

1. Preparing your testimony

After having listened to over a hundred testimonies I realize how powerful or how absolutely obscure they can be. Many of my interviewees' testimonies stirred me deeply; many were clear and, had I not been a Christian, I would have understood how to be reconciled with God. Other testimonies, although meaningful to the individuals, went on and on, and were filled with distracting details. Some used difficult terminology. Non-Christians would have been totally confused.

In order to prepare a clear testimony, you must decide first whether you are a Paul or a Timothy. Paul was converted as an adult, through a dramatic experience as he was traveling to Damascus. Timothy was converted as a child; he was brought up from an early age knowing and loving the Lord. Though different, both were legitimate conversions.

Are you a Paul? If you are a Paul, organize your testimony using Paul's format in Acts 26 as a model. Giving about two minutes to each part, answer these questions:

1. What was your life like before you met Jesus Christ?
   Paul: (Acts 26:9-11) He told how he had opposed Jesus and persecuted Christians, even to their deaths.
   You: What were you like when you were in darkness? What were your interests? Your feelings?

2. How did you meet Jesus Christ?
   Paul: (Acts 26:12-18) He told how he was struck down by a blazing light. Jesus confronted him, showed him He was Lord and that He had come to rescue people from sin and the power of Satan.
   You: How did you hear who Jesus is, why He came, and how

you needed to respond to Him? In other words, this part of your testimony should include a clear presentation of the gospel. Your listener should understand how he or she could become a Christian.

3. What has your life been like since you met Jesus Christ?
Paul: (Acts 26:19-23) Paul was changed. Instead of persecuting Christians he joined them, preaching the gospel. His life was filled with peace and an inextinguishable joy.
You: How has knowing Jesus changed you? What are your interests now? Your goals? Your feelings?

Paul did not get hung up on distracting details. His purpose in giving his testimony was not to draw attention to himself, but to focus his listeners' attention on Jesus and their need for Him.

Are you a Timothy? If you were raised in a Christian home, if you received Jesus as a little child, you probably weren't struck with a lightning bolt as Paul was. But you know with certainty that Jesus Christ is your Savior and Lord of your life. Timothy wouldn't have been able to give a dramatic "life before Christ" presentation; he might not have been able to name the day and time he received Christ. But Timothy's testimony would include a presentation of the gospel and an explanation of what knowing Jesus Christ now means to him. Your testimony should have two parts:

1. Who is Jesus, why did He come, and how must a person respond to Him?
Timothy: He might have explained that from the time he was very young his grandmother and mother explained to him that Jesus was God and that He had come to take his punishment for the bad things he had done. He might have said that he had asked Jesus to forgive him and to come into his life.
You: Whether or not you remember how the gospel was explained isn't really important. This is your opportunity to explain it in terms even a very young child could understand.

2. What does knowing Jesus Christ mean to you today?
Timothy: He might have said that his life was purposeful be-

cause of Jesus. He might have said how glad he was to travel
with Paul so he could tell others about the One who can save us
from sin and from the wrath of God, and assure us of heaven.
He might have described the joy of fellowship and peace amid
persecution.

You: How has knowing Jesus shaped your attitude toward
yourself, toward others, toward life, toward death? What are
some specific ways He is helping you today?

The purpose of a testimony is not to give your listener a
glimpse into you, but into Jesus. Don't obscure Him with a
flood of autobiographical details. Your listener's attention
should be focused on Jesus and the cross.

What If You're Not Sure?

Some people are uncertain whether they are a Paul or a
Timothy. Perhaps they were raised in a Christian home but had
a time of backsliding or serious doubt. Perhaps they remember
receiving Jesus a number of times and aren't sure *when* their
conversion was genuine. People like this are often plagued by
doubts concerning their salvation.

If that is true for you, here's some advice. It's not important
to know when the first time you received Christ was, but the
last time. In other words, when did you finally trust Him for your
salvation? Second, when giving your testimony, don't muddle
the vision of Jesus with distracting details of your confusion.
You don't need to lead your listener through the maze of your
gradual revelation. Move quickly into sharing the gospel and
then note a few specific things about what knowing Jesus
means to you today.

Presenting the Gospel

Another way to share Christ is to skip your testimony and go
right into a presentation of the gospel. Be honest and straightforward. Tell your friend you would like to take a few minutes
and share the central message of the Bible with him. Ask him
if he'd be willing to listen and then give you his reaction to it.

This is a bold approach, yet it is gentle because you are first asking permission.

Any presentation of the gospel should include the following four points:

1. God's nature (He is holy)
2. Man's problem (sinfulness and separation from God)
3. God's solution (Jesus died to take our punishment)
4. Man's response (repentance, faith, commitment)

Make it visual. A visual presentation of the gospel is an aid in clarification. Seeing as well as hearing helps people to concentrate. One woman from Tulsa told me about the impact a flannelgraph presentation had on her:

> One day one of the women in my Bible study brought cut-outs and a large flannelboard. With this she showed us the great gulf that separated human beings from God. Then she showed us how Jesus was the only way back. Suddenly I understood. I realized I needed personally to receive Him as my Savior. Since then I've used the flannelgraph in teaching other groups and it's been very effective. I guess we are all children at heart.

A flannelgraph may not always be handy, but the same presentation can be done with a pen and paper.

Make it scriptural. The Word has power. The Word is the sword of the Spirit. I had to laugh as one black pro football player told me:

> When Jack was quoting Bible verses to me I told him, "I don't believe the Bible is accurate." But he kept on quoting and I was convicted. It's like this: If I was cornered by a killer in a dark alley and all I had was a knife, I sure wouldn't throw down my knife even if he told me he didn't believe in it. I'd know my knife had power no matter what he said. It's the same with the Word.

If your friend has a Bible, or if you have a Bible to give to him, mark the verses so he can return to them later. You might want to keep your verses all in Romans so it will be easier for him to find them. Another practical tool is a well-written tract. It's something your friend can look over later again and again. The Word has power.

Your Attitude

The first few times I presented the gospel to another person I was self-conscious and flustered. I rushed through it, stammering and perspiring. If some sort of comic relief appeared, I welcomed it. I was thinking primarily about myself, not about my friend's great need for Jesus. I was thinking about the impression I was making, not about the message. Here I was telling the most important thing my friend could ever hear, a message that could make an eternal difference, and I was worried about what that person was thinking of *me.*

Have you memorized some verses to explain the gospel? Don't spout them off as if you're participating in a memory drill. This may be the first time your listener has heard these words. J. I. Packer reminds us that our purpose is to "make people think, and think hard about God—and about themselves in relation to God."[1] It may be the first or only time your listener will hear the gospel, so proclaim it clearly as you should (Col. 4:4).

Be sure to define terms like "repentance" and "faith." As Scott's friend described at the beginning of this chapter, if we tell our listeners to "put off the old nature and crucify the flesh," we leave them in a daze.

"Repentance" means asking God for forgiveness and then turning from your old way of life. Instead of living for yourself, you determine to live for Jesus. Every day you make Him the Lord of your life by asking "What do you want me to do and how do you want me to live today?"

"Faith" means placing your trust in Jesus. You need to believe that He paid the price for your sins, that He was raised from the dead, and that through Him you are reconciled to God. It means claiming Jesus as your personal Savior.

Following is a visual presentation of the gospel. Practice this (or another presentation you are comfortable with) until you can explain the gospel clearly.

This example can be demonstrated with your hands and a flat object such as a book.

1. (God's nature) Stretch your left hand up in the air, over your head, to represent God. Say, "God is perfect and holy. He loves us deeply, but He cannot even look on sin. According to the Bible, His character demands justice. He must punish wrongdoing." *Make a fist.*

2. (Man's problem) Hold your right hand out, palm up, to represent man. Say, "Though man was made in God's image, pure and perfect, because of Adam's fall every human being is sinful by nature and practice (Rom. 3:23). Everyone has offended God, has fallen short of God's standard, and deserves to be punished."

3. (God's solution) Take a flat object and place on top of open palm to represent Jesus. Say, "In His great love for us, God gave His only Son to pay the penalty for our sin. Romans 5:8-9 says that 'God demonstrates his own love for us in this: While we were still sinners, Christ died for us. Since we have now been justified by his blood, how much more shall we be saved from God's wrath (anger) through him!' "

4. (Our response) Say, "It's not enough for me to understand why Jesus died on the cross. I must respond personally to this news." *Take flat object away and hit open palm with fist.* "If I reject Christ, God's anger will fall on me." *Now replace flat object on palm and hit it with fist.* "If I receive Christ and He becomes my Lord, God's anger will fall on Jesus instead. 2 Corinthians 5:21 assures us that 'God made him who had no sin to be sin for us, so that in him we might become the righteousness of God.' And Romans 10:9 promises 'If you confess with your mouth [that] Jesus is Lord, and believe in your heart that God raised him from the dead, you will be saved.' "

Again, at this point, I would define my terms. I would explain briefly what salvation means and what it means to acknowledge Christ as Lord.

As I shared this presentation with a church-going neighbor the other day, she watched me intently and then said, with astonishment, "I never really understood that before. I know we are told: 'Jesus died for our sins.' But I never really understood how it worked."

Sharing the Gospel

Now you're ready. You can present the gospel clearly. Don't be surprised if the Lord gives you an opportunity to share what you've prepared very soon. The day after my husband Steve completed a Campus Crusade training course on how to share one's faith, a fellow doctor walked up to him and said, "Steve, why is it that you are so peaceful all the time?"

They went into Steve's office and Steve led his friend to the Lord. "The whole incident seemed right out of a Bill Bright movie!" Steve told me later. I believe it happened because the Lord knew that Steve was prepared.

Terri

I met Terri for the first time when she brought her children to our Vacation Bible School. We'd never seen her before, but she asked if there was anything she could do to help. She was immediately given a job with a craft project. After we'd gotten acquainted, I invited Terri to our women's Bible study, and she accepted. The second time she came to Bible study she caught up with me afterward in the parking lot and said, "Dee, I really need to talk to somebody about the things we've been studying."

Now that day I felt as if I didn't have any room in my schedule. My house was a disaster, and we were expecting company for an early dinner. But I heard the Spirit's soft prompting: "Invite her over." I offered her a yogurt and tea lunch and she said, "That's my favorite!"

Terri poured out her story to me. About a month ago she had begun seeking God. She prayed and asked God to reveal Himself to her. That very day Jehovah's Witnesses came to her door and she assumed this was an answer to her prayer. She began to meet with them. That same week she received my invitation to the women's Bible study. This too might be an answer to her prayer. Now, she was bewildered by the conflicting things she was hearing from the Jehovah's Witnesses and our Bible study. Who was right? Whom should she believe? She had decided to drop either our study or meeting with the Witnesses, but first she wanted to talk to me. What if I had put her off until I could have served her chicken salad and blueberry muffins in a tidy house?

Terri and I prayed together. We looked into the Word together. Terri decided to stop meeting with the Witnesses. Soon after that she received the Lord and bloomed into a beautiful Christian.

It's not always easy to hear the Spirit's voice, to recognize the opportunities He provides. Often we live at a pace that prevents us from being tuned in, from being sensitive. After church one Sunday I was quizzing our four-year-old on what she had learned in Sunday school.

Sally: "We learned that Jesus talks to us."

I: "Oh? How does He talk to us, honey?"

Sally: "He has a still small voice."

I: (Speechless, amazed at my daughter's understanding of this abstract concept; perhaps she was going to be a spiritual giant.)

Sally: "He talks very, very softly" (reflective pause). "That's why I can't hear Him."

I could picture Sally lying on her bed straining to hear Jesus and deciding His voice was too quiet. I feel that way too sometimes, yet He really does speak. I hear His prompting, but only when I am walking closely with Him. The more I am in His Word and in His presence, consciously seeking and expecting to hear Him "break into my day," the greater the chance that I will. The closer we are to Him, the more likely it is that people will come to us with clues that show they are seeking Him.

Take the Initiative

People will come to you. Your responsibility in sharing Christ, however, does not consist only in being ready, in sitting back and waiting. You must also take the initiative in sharing Christ. Jesus commanded, "Go into all the world and preach the good news to all creation" (Mark 16:15). Maybe you and a friend have talked about spiritual things a few times, but you've never really gotten to the Good News. How can you lead into sharing the gospel?

It's not nearly as difficult as Satan would like you to believe. You simply ask permission. With candor and gentleness you ask permission to talk about the central issue of Christ. I'd like to share two stories with you. These Christians were straightforward with their friends and won them to Christ.

Linda and Jim

Larry developed a friendship with Linda and Jim through their mutual interest in Little League. They watched several games together, talking and laughing. As time passed, a friendship developed that was important to all of them. One day Larry asked Linda and Jim if he could come over some evening and share some things about Jesus that meant a great deal to him. He took the initiative in sharing the gospel with them. They *heard* and responded. Linda and Jim told me that they appreciated Larry's sincere forthright approach.

Gordon

"I was a pagan sailor," Gordon told me. "Marge was a Christian." As Marge was getting to know Gordon, she began to pray for him earnestly. She also practiced presenting the gospel clearly. "She memorized Scripture like crazy," Gordon said. Then one night "after a lot of listening and tactful questions, she asked me if she could share the basic gospel message with me." Marge had done her homework well, and Gordon understood what he needed to do to be reconciled with God. Marge then invited him to trust Jesus as his Savior and Lord. He told me his first response was, "No, I think I'd better think about it."

Marge shook her head. "You'll never do it."

Gordon smiled. "That's all it took." He received the Savior that night.

Don't Be Mysterious

How often have you heard someone say, "Well, I've never really talked about Jesus with my neighbor, but he knows where I stand." Kathy told me how she used to feel about her mysterious Christian neighbor:

> When I lived in Pennsylvania several of the women in the neighborhood would get together for coffee and conversation. We were very young and didn't know how to take Mandy. Every once in a while she would make some mysterious religious comment and the conversation would come to a halt. It wasn't that we weren't interested, which perhaps is what she thought; it was that we didn't understand what she was talking about. I remember one time she mentioned some decision she and her husband were facing and she said: "We put it to prayer." That's all she said and then everybody was silent. At the time I thought it was interesting that they prayed about things like that, and I wished she would elaborate, but she never did—and nobody knew how to begin to draw her out.

Christians are often so afraid of being offensive that they opt for making brief vague comments, hoping it will lead to something. Wouldn't it be better to state things more forthrightly and then ask if we're coming on too strong?

Peter and John prayed, "Enable your servants to speak your word with great boldness" (Acts 4:29). We need to pray that too. Instead of beating around the bush, we must openly and gently ask permission to share the central message.

Try This:

• Prepare a visual presentation of the gospel with three memorized verses. Go over it with a Christian friend and ask that person to critique you truthfully. Ask your friend, "If you had never heard the gospel before, would you have understood my presentation? Would you know how to become a Christian? How could I make it clearer?"

● Pray for three friends whom you'd like to see come to Christ. Invite one of them over this week and ask permission to share the gospel.

9
Encouraging a Response to God

*We had talked a lot, Sherri and I. I had so many
questions and she had done her best to answer them using
Scripture. One day she asked, "Is there any reason
why you couldn't commit your life to Christ?" I kind
of gulped and thought, "There really isn't any barrier."*
—a woman from Tennessee

*In their rush to acquire things, people sometimes
seem like mice in a cage running to make the wheel go
round and round. There's lots of activity, but
they aren't going anywhere. Somehow we have to arrest
that cyclic action and make them stop and think about life.*
—Warfield Munce, a missionary to Japan

WE WANT PEOPLE TO COME to God because they are sincerely
responding to His calling—not because they are yielding to
human pressure. Manipulation and pressure in evangelism are
outside God's will. I can remember being asked to sing ten
choruses of "Almost Persuaded" at the close of an evangelistic
message and being immensely relieved I had brought no one
with me. Manipulated "conversions" tend to be spurious. (I am
especially concerned that people who work with children exercise caution in giving invitations, since children are so easily
manipulated.)

Many Christians, in reaction to high-pressure tactics, fail to do
anything to encourage others to respond to God. But it is scripturally legitimate, and it may be pivotal, to encourage our
friends to do that. Procrastinators by nature, people need to be
encouraged to respond to God while He is calling. It makes

sense not to put off responding since, although no one (while alive) is outside the reach of God, it does seem that those who harden their heart to His early calls are less likely to hear Him later. When we know a friend has understood the gospel and the cost of commitment, we should encourage a response.

What is the difference between pressure and encouragement? Pressure badgers. Encouragement plants a question in the listener's mind and leaves the rest up to the Holy Spirit.

Paul encouraged people to respond. He said that because "we know what it is to fear the Lord, we try to persuade men" (2 Cor. 5:11). Paul personally confronted King Agrippa by asking him if he believed the prophets and by telling him that he was praying for him to become a Christian.

Some of the people whom I interviewed told me that when they were asked if they wished to make a decision for Christ they responded negatively. But the question stayed in their mind and later brought them to God. The Spirit didn't let them forget the question.

Possible Questions

Just as there is no pat formula for presenting the gospel, neither is there a single question for encouraging a response. But because most of us get clammy when we even consider asking a friend if she or he would like to respond to Jesus, it is helpful to have some questions ready in our minds. Paul Little said that if we're prepared with something, at least we won't black out. A progression he suggested is:

1. Have you ever personally trusted Christ, or are you still on the way?
2. How far along the way are you?
3. Would you like to become a real Christian and be sure?[1]

Bill Bright, founder of Campus Crusade, has given people a tract (the Van Dusen letter) and asked them to read it. Then he asks:

1. Does this make sense to you?
2. Would you like to receive Christ?

Another question Campus Crusade often uses is: Is there any reason why you couldn't commit your life to Christ? Two people I interviewed told me that that question was helpful in encouraging their decision. One woman I quoted at the opening of this chapter. The other was my sister Sally.

When Sally was teaching Spanish at Iowa State University she asked her class to write an essay in Spanish on "Who My Best Friend Is—And Why." One of her students wrote that her best friend was Jesus. Intrigued by the essay, Sally asked this student if she would do some babysitting for her. Sally said Bonny often left tracts on the coffee table and then later asked Sally if she had read them and had any questions. Finally Bonny summoned the courage to ask Sally: "Is there any reason why you couldn't commit your life to Christ?"

That question kept coming back to Sally through the evening and the next day. It was a tool used by the Holy Spirit to clarify her thoughts and bring her to repentance and commitment.

If Your Friend Is Ready
The first time I asked someone if she would like to receive Christ, she said, "I think so—yes." And then, "Yes, I would." My reaction was sheer panic. I had almost hoped she would say no because I felt so inadequate. But like a medical student delivering his or her first baby, I fumbled through the birth. Then I realized that that "baby" would have been born no matter how unskilled I was. Still, it's good to be prepared so that both your friend and you experience as little trauma as possible.

Begin by being sure your friend understands the gospel. Then encourage your friend to say his or her own prayer. Although it's not always inappropriate, there's a danger in praying for them or having them pray after you (you might be forcing a premature birth). You want to be sure that it is that person's sincere desire to make this commitment. Assure your friend that the important thing is one's heart, not the eloquence of one's words. God will understand if he or she is repentant and has faith in Christ.

It might be helpful to read over Psalm 51 together, or to tell your friend how you prayed when you received Christ. If your friend would be more comfortable praying without you there, allow that freedom. (Most of the people I interviewed prayed on their own.)

Getting Through to the Apathetic

Some friends are not receptive. Perhaps they've listened politely to you, but their heart doesn't really seem to be there. When you make a comment about something spiritual, they look at you blankly. Football, food, fashion: those subjects bring a spark to their eyes. How, you wonder, can I get them to think about what life is all about? How can I get them to look up beyond this earth to God?

I can think of three ways to challenge, to soften, apathetic hearts. Two I've mentioned before; the third is new:

1. Pray.
2. Persist in loving them into the kingdom.
3. Provoke their thoughts with questions and the Word.

1. Pray. By ourselves we are powerless to draw a person to the Lord. J. I. Packer has said that realizing "we depend wholly on God to make our witness effective should drive us to prayer."[2]

Holly invited all her neighbors in her rural Iowa neighborhood to a Bible study. They all came. "How," I asked Holly, "do you account for such a great response?" "I prayed," she explained. "For six months I prayed persistently. I prayed for each one of those women every day. Then I invited them."

2. Persist. Jim Petersen tells how a comment made by a professor made a permanent mark on him. Dr. Bob Smith said to Jim, "You know, ninety percent of evangelism is love."[3]

Love melts hard hearts. Listen to the following story:

> When Barb first moved into our neighborhood, the neighbors thought she was strange. She had this bumpersticker that said "Think Jesus." That really got tongues wagging. We all considered ourselves to be Christians, yet no one talked about the Lord; our conversations were always about superficial things. Barb was different. She was also very generous, very loving. In time we felt a little ashamed of the way we'd talked about her behind her back. She was always so ready to help, to give of herself. Seven years later, Barb had evangelized the whole block. How different we are now!

Barb's experience illustrates the advice Peter gave:

> "But in your hearts set apart Christ as Lord. Always be prepared to give an answer to everyone who asks you to give the reason for the hope that you have. But do this with gentleness and respect, keeping a clear conscience, so that those who speak maliciously against your good behavior in Christ may be ashamed of their slander" (1 Pet. 3:15-16).

People who are apathetic about spiritual things are likely to be critical of Christians. But love can melt hard hearts, make them ashamed, and draw them to the One who has provided that love.

3. Be provocative. Some people are not interested in spiritual things because they have been persuaded that true fulfillment lies in earthly things: money, pleasure, power. They may be unimpressed with what we say about our faith. "That's terrific for you, but I have my own ideas on how to be happy."

We need some provocative questions that will cause our apathetic friends to think about the reality of God. We can also do this by using the Word, the "sword of the Spirit." Is it possible to interact with such people without being offensive? I think so. I'd like you to meet two individuals who were successful in making the apathetic turn to Jesus Christ.

Sally

Sally is my model in evangelism. She is my sister, and she led me to the Lord. She is a warm, loving, articulate woman, who was a very serious child. We used to kid her that she was born with a frown, immediately questioning why she was on earth and what she was to do with her life. Our dad tells of a time he laid linoleum in our basement. Sally sat on the steps, tears streaming down her cheeks. "None of my friends have linoleum. Why do we need linoleum? With so many hungry people in the world, why are we spending money on linoleum?" But though we tease Sally about her outlook on life, I'm forever grateful that she took God seriously.

A year after her conversion she decided it was time to visit Steve and me. During that visit Sally literally followed me around the house with an open Bible and asked me questions. "Who do you think Jesus is?" "Why do you think Jesus died on the cross?" "Did you know He asks you to give Him your whole life?"

Sally's questions got my mind spinning. She made me think hard about God. As we began to dialogue, Sally did her best to show me scriptural answers to my questions. She was using the sword of the Spirit to stir my apathetic mind.

Warfield

Warfield is an American missionary in Japan, one of the world's most difficult mission fields. Less than one percent of the people claim to be Christians. Converts to Christianity are often persecuted. (One young man, who received Christ through International Students Inc. while in the U.S., was told by his wife and father not to return.[4]) In addition, Japan has become even more materialistic than America (though I find that hard to imagine)! Men spend practically all their waking hours on the job. There is little time for family or spiritual life. Yet Warfield has found a way to provoke people's interest in the gospel of Jesus Christ, especially as a result of his study of Ecclesiastes.

For example, he had a friend whom he wished to interest in

the gospel. This man was very busy and hadn't seemed particularly interested in spiritual things. Warfield said, "Somehow, I wanted to get beyond surface conversation and grab this man's attention by finding something that was close to his heart."

Ecclesiastes shows us that families are often important to unbelievers. The man who has no family may say, "For whom am I toiling?" (Eccles. 4:8). But the person who has a spouse and children finds some comfort, some meaning, in them. One purpose such a person can see is to provide for their family.

Warfield's friend talked about his teenage daughter with obvious pride and affection. So Warfield began there. He showed his friend an article about the suicides of two junior high school girls who planned their deaths six months ahead of time yet neither family suspected anything.

Warfield told his friend he was sharing this with him so he would stop and think about life. They began to talk about suicide, an alarming problem in Japan, and about why these two girls, in particular, took their lives.

One of the things the men talked about was that appearances can be deceiving. "Even in laughter the heart may ache" (Prov. 14:13). These teenage girls seemed to be getting along fine, yet they took their lives. Warfield said, "People can have very pleasant relationships and yet not really be heart to heart." His friend confided that he wondered why he had to be so busy.

Warfield asked him, "Does your daughter really know why she's living? Does she have a purpose for life?" At that point a friend of Warfield gave a bit of his own personal testimony. That was as far as they went that evening, but the next day the Japanese friend called and thanked Warfield for their conversation. He said he had gone home and, though it was after midnight, had discussed these things with his wife. He told Warfield he wanted to get together again soon. His interest had been provoked.

My sister Sally and Warfield both used questions to make their listeners think. Questions can be a tool of the Holy Spirit (Jesus used them all the time). It's a lot harder to drift off during a conversation when questions are being asked than it is during a monologue. Sally asked, "Who do you think Jesus is?" and "Do you think the disciples would have been willing to give their lives for a lie?" Warfield asked, "Does your daughter really know why she's living? Does she have a purpose in life?"

They were both prepared with Scripture to answer the questions they themselves had posed. Sally led me through the four spiritual laws, an explanation of the gospel published by Campus Crusade. Warfield's friend gave his testimony, laced with Scripture. The Word has power to awaken the apathetic.

Persist in prayer. Persist in love. Use questions and use the Word.

Try This:
- Carry some good tracts in your wallet. Memorize one question that could be used as a tool to encourage a response to God.
- Do you have an apathetic friend? Prepare two questions about Jesus that might start that person thinking. Be prepared with scriptural answers.

Part II

Finding-Keeping

*Finding: Making friends
with non-Christians
and loving them
into the kingdom*

*Keeping: Teaching those
who seem to believe
to obey all
that Jesus commanded*

10
Conversion: A Process

*As He kept Abraham waiting twenty-five years
for the birth of his son, so He often keeps Christians waiting
for things that they long to see, such as the conversion
of their friends. We need patience, then, if we are to do our
part in helping others towards faith. And the way
for us to develop that patience is to learn to live in terms of
our knowledge of the free and gracious sovereignty
of God . . . and, the knowledge that God is sovereign in
grace, and that we are impotent to win souls,
should make us pray, and keep us praying.*
—J. I. Packer[1]

IF WE LOSE HEART because we don't see a response shortly after we share the gospel, we don't understand conversion. Jesus compared conversion to planting wheat:

> "The Kingdom of God is like this. A man scatters seed in his field. He sleeps at night, is up and about during the day, and all the while the seeds are sprouting and growing. Yet he does not know how it happens. The soil itself makes the plants grow and bear fruit; first the tender stalk appears, then the head, and finally the head full of grain" (Mark 4:26-28, TEV).

Since that parable can help us to understand conversion, let us examine it carefully.

Conversion: A Mystery
First, it seems evident that conversion is a mystery. The only One who really understands exactly when and how new life

begins is the Creator of that life. People I interviewed were often
uncertain about when God's Spirit took hold of them. Eventually they knew a new spiritual life was there, but it was hard for
them to pinpoint its beginnings. Let me illustrate with Tom's
story:

> It's hard for me to tell you *when* I received Christ. You see, I don't
> really know. When I was in high school I stepped on a Youth for
> Christ bus and one of the leaders asked if I wanted to receive Christ.
> I prayed with him, and it was a very quick incident in my life. But
> nothing was changed. Then there was the time in the service that
> my bunkmate asked me to help him review some of his memory
> verses. Then he asked me if I wanted to receive Christ. I hesitated
> and he didn't push. But before he went to sleep he leaned down
> and said, "If you *do* want Jesus in your life, wake me up. Even if
> it's the middle of the night." That spooked me, but it made me
> think. I lay there thinking. The next morning I told him I did want
> Christ in my life. Maybe that's when my commitment was real. And
> yet it wasn't until I got back to the States and was involved with The
> Navigators that I began to see some real changes in my life.

Sometimes we evangelicals legalistically insist that Christians
be able to name the date and time of their new birth. Not every
one can, but that does not mean they have not been born
again. One woman said:

> I know some people would disagree with me but I think the day His
> Spirit entered my life was the day I asked my sister if I could read
> some of her Christian pamphlets. I did not yet fully understand why
> Jesus had died, nor had I repented. But that day was a turning point
> because finally I was yielding to God. A great hunger for spiritual
> truth began that day which I can't explain in any other way except
> that His Spirit had come in.

Underneath the ground seeds may be sprouting and growing
secretly, yet it may be months before anything appears above
ground. I received Jesus as my Savior a week after my sister
Sally's visit, but she didn't find out until a year later. People who
care about the salvation of another can become discouraged. Is
anything actually happening? Should we persist, or give up?

Jesus also told the Parable of the Sower. I think we can be encouraged that the seed sprouted in three out of the four soils. Yet, on the other hand, only one soil bore long-term fruit. What made the difference? Obviously part of it was the condition of the soil.

There is also the mystery of the Spirit, without whom nothing can happen. What part does the farmer play? In this world, the patient care of a farmer can make a crucial difference in whether or not a crop succeeds. Is the same true in the kingdom of heaven? It is a mystery. What we know is that we are to persist and not grow weary.

Conversion: Patience Needed

Almost all of the people I interviewed needed time to consider after being asked if they would like to respond to Jesus. A book about Jim Elliot records these thoughts:

> Personally, I wasn't "saved" all at once, but took some years coming into my present settled convictions about the truth of God. So why should I demand that conversion be immediate in all others? Christ healed men differently. Some, in absentia—He spoke a word, and there was a lightning-fast reaction. Others He touched, spat upon, made clay, spoke to and questioned, then when they saw men "as trees walking" He went through the whole process again. Let not him who accepts light in an instant despise him who gropes months in the shadows. [2]

We who know the Lord may find it difficult to comprehend how others, after seeing Him, could put Him off. Perhaps they are holding onto something they think He will ask them to give up. How, we ask, could they possibly see *that,* whatever it is, as of greater worth than Jesus, than their soul?

John Brekke, who was with The Navigators in North Dakota, told me he used to be terribly discouraged when, after answering many questions to a student's satisfaction, the student was still reluctant to commit himself to Christ. "But then I realized," he explained,

having a relationship with God . . . takes time. Let's say, for example, that you had met your future spouse last night. How would
you feel if I began to pressure you, saying, "This is the ideal guy
for you. You should marry him immediately." I think you'd be
pretty hesitant.

A commitment to Christ is the biggest decision a person will
ever make. If we have presented the full picture and asked our
friend to count the cost, we should not be surprised if he or she
needs some time to think. Gradual conversion is much more
common than sudden conversion. Dr. James Engel explains
that conversion may seem sudden, yet it is the culmination of
a process.[3]

In this context of gradual conversion I'd like to reiterate the
point that *finding* and *keeping* are a continuous process rather
than two distinct steps. Finding means making friends with non-
Christians and loving them into the kingdom. Keeping means
teaching those who seem to believe to obey all that Jesus has
commanded. Since it is so difficult to tell when someone really
is in the kingdom, we should move right on to teaching those
who seem to believe. By not judging we'll put no one on the
defensive. Those who are still unsaved may discover they are
unsaved. Those who are saved will grow strong. After you have
sown the seed, keep on!

Conversion: Persistence Needed

Persistence means not giving up on your friend, whether there
is sign of spiritual life or not. Keep on praying, keep on loving,
keep on sharing, keep on inviting. Treat that person as if he or
she is interested, for really they may be. J. I. Packer says, "We
cannot hope for success unless we are prepared to persevere
with people."[4]

If we are loving, if our friends know we genuinely care about
them, they won't be offended by our persistence. I often have
the feeling I'm hounding someone if I keep on inviting them to
Bible study, yet many of the people I interviewed told me they
were grateful for a friend's persistence. Marlis told me:

Barb asked me to join a Bible study with her but Bible study just scared the daylights out of me—I thought that was for theologians and really smart people. So I said no. Then she started asking me to Christian Women's Club. She was very persistent, and very loving. When you have a Christian in your neighborhood it's a little overpowering because you can't lie to them all the time, thinking up reasons why you can't go somewhere. Finally I went to Christian Women's Club and for the first time in my life I heard a woman give a testimony of the reality of Jesus Christ in her life. No one had ever talked to me about anything personal like that before. I went back to more monthly meetings. Then Barb invited me to another Bible study and that time I went.

If you were raised in a Christian home it may be difficult to comprehend the web of darkness, of lies, that Satan casts over unbelievers. Paul says they are in the "trap of the devil" (2 Tim. 2:26).

Howard Hendricks has observed that the average person tends to go through three stages in the process of embracing an idea: resistance, tolerance, and acceptance.[5] The first time you are invited to a Bible study or told about Jesus or hear a testimony, you tend to resist. A natural reaction to something new is to put your defenses up. It takes time for a person's eyes to get adjusted to light. So be patient. All growth takes time.

Try This:
● In *How to Give Away Your Faith,* Paul Little deals with the seven questions most frequently asked on secular campuses, questions like "What about the heathen?" and "Isn't the Bible full of errors?" Read his book and practice answering those questions. Work with a Christian partner.

11
Ways to Reach Out to Others

*When the crusade came to Portland a girl in my office
invited several of us over for supper and then to
hear Billy Graham. We decided to go—sort of as a lark.*
—Pam, a foster mother from Oregon

*I went because I was curious to see what kind of
squirrelly people studied the Bible . . . their love kept me
coming back, and, in time, the Word brought me to faith.*
—a former skeptic from Minden, Nebraska

MANY OF THE PEOPLE I interviewed received Jesus after attending a Christian seminar, retreat, or evangelistic meeting. How did they happen to attend? They went because a friend invited them. Rarely had they wandered into those events on their own.

Too often we think that we are fulfilling our evangelistic responsibility when our church rents a film or invites a gospel singer. It isn't enough to prepare a three-course candlelit dinner, you must invite the guests.

Invite Your Friends to Special Events
Statistics support the importance of personal invitations. For example, when Win Arn researched the Billy Graham Seattle

Crusade it was found that the great majority of those who made a response of some type were brought to the meeting by someone else.[1]

I met Pam in Oregon. She had that gentle and quiet spirit which comes from deep contentment in the Lord. She told me that when the Billy Graham Crusade came to Portland, she probably wouldn't have gone except that a girl in her office invited several of her co-workers.

> On the way home in the car several of the others were laughing about the whole thing—but I was deep in thought. The things that had been said had the ring of truth. I realized I wanted to go back and hear more.

Pam did go back and responded to Christ at the next meeting.

Truth in a Fresh Way

A few of the people I interviewed had been in a strong evangelical setting for many months or even years, yet they hadn't heard or hadn't responded to the truth. But when they went to a special event, God's light broke through. Mick, a building contractor, told me:

> I'd been going with my wife to a Bible-preaching church for more than five years. However, it wasn't until I attended Bill Gothard's Basic Youth Conflicts that I received Christ. He presented an opportunity to make a commitment and I realized I knew what he was talking about—I'd heard it many times—but I had never said "Yes, I do want this relationship." I saw my sinful nature that day and I realized I needed a Savior.

Bill Gothard presented the same gospel that had been presented many times in Mick's church, but something about the different setting had an impact. We're all different, and perhaps that's why the Spirit moves in various ways. You and I might find a particular church very stimulating, yet someone else is able to tune out Sunday after Sunday. Perhaps that person needs to hear the truth in a fresh way.

When a special event comes to town or to your church, pray

for the Lord to guide your thinking about whom to invite. If the event has great value and the people you first invite make excuses, go into the highways and byways and invite others. Don't let these opportunities slip by.

Keep on Inviting

Before I did these interviews I was hesitant to invite people more than once to something. If they said no the first time, I left them alone. They just weren't interested in spiritual things, I thought. Now I am convinced that gentle persistence is important. Listen to these comments from my interviews:

> The idea of Bible study scared me and when Audrey invited me I told her my schedule was very tight. But as I got to know her during the next year, I wondered if I should have gone. I thought, if she asks me again, I'll try it. She did.

> My mother-in-law hounded me to attend a local evangelistic meeting. I went to get her off my back. I didn't plan to go back. But the next day my twelve-year-old nephew, my fishing partner, called. He asked if I could please take him to the second meeting. How could I say no? I met the Lord that night.

> When Maureen invited me to Christian Women's Club I wasn't sure I wanted to go—I was almost relieved I had a dentist's appointment! But she acted as if she thought it was something I would really enjoy, and she told me they had babysitting. The next month, when she called again, I thought, "I'm just going to give it a try!"

God didn't give up on the Jewish people. He sent messenger after messenger. Jesus explained to the disciples time after time that He was going to be crucified. If the Lord keeps putting forth His message, so should we.

It's unrealistic to expect a person to respond eagerly to our first invitation. It's also unrealistic to expect a single evangelistic sermon to open people's eyes fully. We must be persistent.

Begin an Evangelistic Bible Study

There is power in evangelistic Bible studies. In the best studies, three elements combine to open blinded eyes: the Word, the fellowship, and the continuity.

First, there is the Word itself, the sword of the Spirit. In an inductive study, people are digging into the Bible for themselves, not simply hearing it and possibly tuning out. They discover what it says. They find applications for their lives. As Naomi Wright has observed, digging the truths out yourself is comparable to finding gold with your own pickax—it's a lot more exciting than hearing about someone else's discovery.[2]

Second, there is the loving fellowship. People keep on coming because of the atmosphere of caring. Not only does love impress them as being the mark of something real, they want to know that kind of love. Bobbie, the former skeptic from Minden, told me she was amazed at the love shown her when she visited a Bible study group.

> I was very antagonistic. I said, "Do you *really* believe this stuff? Do you really believe it?" They didn't argue, they just kept on loving me. And they weren't putting it on—it was real.

I laughed as Rochelle told me her initial reaction to her Bible study's prayer and share time:

> I didn't say it out loud, but I couldn't believe they actually thought God was going to hear their requests. I thought, "They think they can pray these things into happening!" When they asked me if I had any requests I never knew what to say—but it did touch me that they seemed to care about me and my life.

Rochelle kept coming back and today she knows that God hears her requests.

Then, third, there is the continuity of meeting week after week, creating circumstances where the light can dawn slowly.

Considering what a powerhouse evangelistic studies are, why aren't there more of them? Why are most Bible studies made up of Christians rather than being truly evangelistic? I can think of two reasons.

Christians lack confidence. They don't think they could

"teach" a beginners' study, so they join an already existing group. Or they lack the knowhow to get a group going. They think they could lead one if they could get one started, but they don't know how to interest others in coming.

Too many Christians believe they should have a degree in Greek (or at least a year of Bible college) before they lead a study. The facts are, however, that studies led by those with degrees in Greek are not necessarily good discussions. Many pastors or seminary graduates end up teaching the group instead. And while I believe there is a definite place for teaching and for sermons, it is not in an evangelistic Bible discussion group.

People need to discover the truth and articulate it for themselves. Laypeople often minister better to laypeople than does an expert. As C. S. Lewis explained, "The expert sees the whole subject, by now, in such a different light that he cannot conceive what is really troubling the pupil; he sees a dozen other difficulties which ought to be troubling him but aren't . . . the fellow pupil can help more than the master because he knows less."[3]

The best evangelistic study groups have a leader who is a moderator, not a teacher. The Holy Spirit is the teacher, and it's important to have a leader who won't quench Him. So if you've been holding back because you don't know Greek, or because you don't see yourself as a teacher, consider that you may be perfect for the calling.

How to Do It

How can you interest others in coming to a study? What should you study when they come? There are four "P's" in starting an evangelistic study: prayer, partner, plan, personal invitation.

Prayer. Since no one can come to the Father unless the Holy Spirit draws them, you must pray for the people you plan to invite. Tape their names up somewhere and pray fervently for them.

Partner. A Christian partner to help you isn't a necessity, but an encouragement. That way, two of you are praying, planning, inviting others. Be careful to choose someone who has a heart for non-Christians. Don't choose someone who is apt to monopolize the discussion or push controversial doctrines. If you can't find such a partner, don't be stymied. Go ahead on your own. I predict the Lord will provide someone right within the ranks of your study in a matter of months.

Plan. Decisions need to be made at least a month in advance. You and your partner need to plan whom to invite, what you'll study, when and where you'll begin. Based on my experience, I'd like to make a few suggestions that may help you.

1. The most common mistake Christians make in beginning an evangelistic study is to invite several Christian friends. A study made up of eight Christians and two non-Christians is not an evangelistic study. In fact, the two non-Christians probably will drop out soon because they will feel self-conscious about their lack of knowledge. In an evangelistic study you invite those who have not been in a study before. Make it clear that this is a beginners' study. A beginner's greatest fear is that she or he will be the only one new to the Bible.

2. A studyguide will simplify the discussion leader's job and prove a valuable aid for homework during the week. The inexperienced are unsure of what to look for when reading a passage, and a guide will help them. An inductive studyguide poses questions that will cause students to dig in the biblical text for the answers. Choose a guide that takes a whole book of the Bible or that takes long passages in context. Beginners need to look at whole pictures before they look at pieces. I especially like the Fisherman series (Shaw). InterVarsity Press and Zondervan also have some excellent guides. Most Christian book stores would be happy to have you check out several on approval.

3. Homes provide intimate nonthreatening atmospheres for nondenominational studies. Rotating the home every two weeks can help everyone to feel more involved.

4. Evening groups can usually fend for themselves, but

women's daytime groups need sitters. Women who are home and available for a study are likely to be caring for the children of mothers working at outside jobs. It's tempting to avoid extending an invitation to a woman who is caring for extra children, but that is missing a wonderful opportunity. Not only might this woman be reached, but, through her, the children in her care.

How can you find sitters? Pray for them. Call local churches for the names of women who sit in their nurseries. When I interviewed Mary, a regional coordinator for Friendship Bible Coffees, I asked her how she found babysitters. She said:

> This may not sound practical and down to earth, but God provides them. We make it a matter of prayer and we *always* find one. Sometimes I have to get on the phone and call a lot of people, but if a sitter is needed, we'll find one. And, if the group needs a free sitter, God will provide that.

I suggest that while you are praying for a sitter, you pray for one who could teach the older preschoolers songs, verses, and Bible stories. Bible Study Fellowship (an excellent nationwide study group) has done this and has found it to be a wonderful ministry. James tells us, "You do not have because you do not ask God" (James 4:2b). So ask God for someone who will teach the children. I've had this prayer answered repeatedly.

Right now in the study we have in Kearney, Nebraska, we have three volunteers teaching the children in Bible Club. We found them by praying and then personally asking those women who came to mind. Each had had a desire to serve the Lord in this kind of ministry and accepted enthusiastically.

Personal Invitation

The best way to invite friends to a study is by personal invitation. Remember, non-Christians have many reservations about a Bible study, so they'll be much less likely to come if the invitation is impersonal.

When I moved to Fargo and wanted to have an evangelistic

neighborhood study, the Lord gave me Beth as a Christian partner. Together we walked around the block, knocking on thirty-five doors. Twenty were not at home. At those homes we dropped the invitation into the mailbox. Those were my favorite stops, easy and nonintimidating. But like the invitations dropped from the famous Gospel Blimp,[4] they proved unfruitful. Who did come? The women who already knew Beth or me and who were invited face to face.

Last year in Kearney three other women and I met in June to pray and plan for Fall studies. We had the following invitation printed (figure 6). It was inexpensive and we found it to be an effective tool. Christians were much more at ease about inviting their neighbors and friends when they had this card to give them.

WE INVITE YOU!

Join us in studying God's Word and applying it to our lives.

Group Bible Studies

Non-denominational
Nursery and Bible Club for ages 0-6
Choice of Studies

Come for Coffee, Registration, & Preview
Tuesday, Sept. 7, 10 AM
at the home of
John & Mary Smith, 1406 Fourth Avenue
(map on back)

Studies begin Tuesday, Sept. 28, 9:00-11:15 AM

Figure 6

At the preview meeting forty women signed up for their choice of beginning or intermediate studies. We also had twenty-five children registered for Bible Club. At the end of the first semester, we gave each woman four invitation cards to pass out. Second semester seventy women registered.

Because people are insecure, direct communication gives you an opportunity to reassure them. Let them know you'll all be learning together; they won't be put on the spot or embarrassed.

Anne knew only a few of her neighbors well but wanted to invite them all to her study. She decided to stop in at each neighbor's house and extend a personal invitation to a coffee which would introduce them to a sample study. After telling them about it she left a card with a reminder of the date and time.

Fifteen women came for Anne's sample study. While sitting in front of the fireplace with coffee and cookies, a friend of Anne explained how an adult Bible discussion operated and led a short sample study. After that study, Lorraine said:

> I have learned more this afternoon than from years of jumping around through the Bible by myself. If this is what happens in a Bible study, I'll be there every week.[5]

Try This:
- Many excellent Christian movies are available for rent. Plan to rent four evangelistic films for a series of Friday nights six months from now. Share the vision with your congregation so they can be planning now whom they will invite.
- Pray and plan now for a study you'll start in three months. Consider using one of these guides:

Mark: God in Action (Chuck & Winnie Christensen, Harold Shaw Publishers)
Proverbs & Parables (Dee Brestin, Harold Shaw Publishers)
A Woman's Workshop on Romans (Carolyn Nystrom, Zondervan)

12
Bible Studies That Go and Grow

*When Gwenn invited me to study she said it
would meet every week. I remember thinking, "Every
week? You meet to study the Bible every week? You won't
be seeing me that often!" . . . But this Bible study
is the absolute high point of my week. I think about it all
the time—I'm eager to do the lesson at home
so I can halfway keep up with the others. I'm so blessed
by the discussion, but it's more than that.
I feel loved and cared for by these women. I'd have to
be on my deathbed to miss!*
**—a new Christian commenting on her
first Bible study**

*The easiest part of an evangelistic Bible study
is the study itself. The bigger challenge is to generate the
desire to attend and to sustain the interest over
the long haul.*
—Jim Petersen[1]

YOUR BATTLE IS NOT WON when your neighbors or your co-workers agree to come to the first study. How do you keep them coming?

Encourage Participation
When you have a group of new students who are struggling with the simplest passage, the most tempting thing to do is to answer the questions yourself or to glare at your Christian partner until he or she answers. Remember, people will be much

more excited about discovering things for themselves. Stress that the answers to the questions are in the biblical text. The silence may seem long, but the rewards will be great. If this discussion group turns into a lecture by you, they probably won't be back.

Pray
Don't stop praying now that they've come. During the first few weeks they will be filled with doubts as to whether they should keep coming. Pray harder than ever. One woman said,

> My husband and I nearly dropped out of that study many times—
> we'd talk about it, but then we'd go back. I don't know why we kept
> coming back. I guess God kept us coming back.

Keep in Touch
Jim Petersen suggests that you have some sort of informal interchange between encounters.

> It doesn't take much. In fact, be careful not to overdo it. "Seldom
> set foot in your neighbor's house—too much of you, and he will
> hate you" (Proverbs 25:17). A ten-minute visit is enough time to
> gather some feedback and to verify the time and place of your next
> meeting. But it is essential. And it may be such informal moments
> which open the way for deeper conversations.[2]

You and your partner can divide the list. A phone call, a brief visit—let them know you're thinking of them.

Making a Good Group Even Better
Bible study groups vary greatly. Some are simply glorified coffee klatches, enjoyable, but not too edifying. Some are slow-moving and boring. Many are life-changing and stimulating. We want to be continually striving to make our groups the best they can be. These seven ideas have worked well in my study groups.

1. Give Homework. During the first week you'll need to show the members how to find chapter and verse. Encourage them to use the Bible's table of contents to find the location of specific books. If everyone is doing it, there will be less embarrassment. One woman in a beginners' study kept fumbling through the pages until she finally resorted to the contents page. After a moment, she said, "Good grief! There are four Johns! Why didn't you tell me?"

By doing the lesson together for the first week or two, members will discover that the answers to the questions are in the text. As soon as they discover that principle, and how to find a verse, they are ready for homework.

Assign the lesson ahead of time. You might tell your group that some studies have a rule that members who have not done their lesson are not allowed to talk during the discussion (a severe discipline for a lot of us).

After a few months, begin assigning memory work—a verse a week, word perfect. I like to begin meetings by going around the room and hearing each person's memory work and then their response to it. For example, in a recent study, we were working in 1 John 2. Sherri began with her memorized verse:

> 1 John 2:15. Do not love the world or anything in the world. If anyone loves the world, the love of the Father is not in him. 1 John 2:15.

Then she said, "All this week it's been going round and round in my head, 'Do not love the world! Do not love the world!' That verse puts it so strongly. It says if you love the world, the love of the Father is not in you."

Next, it was Shell's turn. She had chosen a verse from the same passage:

> 1 John 2:17. The world and its desires pass away, but the man who does the will of God lives forever. 1 John 2:17.

"I've been thinking about this verse," Shell said, "as I've been thumbing through the umpteen catalogs that come to my house. All the things in those catalogs are going to pass away. My catalogs have always meant a great deal to me but I think they are a stumbling block in my fellowship with the Lord."

2. Balance the pace. Groups that move too slowly discourage homework. Most studyguide lessons were written to be completed in one session. If your group is finding this difficult, skip a few questions and proceed to the closing application questions. A good leader is alert to a discussion that is moving far afield of the text and will move the group on to the next question. People have all kinds of questions, so it's easy to get off on tangents. If you allow this to happen you'll have a coffee klatch rather than a Bible study.

Though it's a less common problem, some groups move too quickly. Be sure to allow time for silence after questions and comments. This is precious time. The Spirit is teaching and prompting the quieter members to gather courage and share.

3. Draw out shyer members. Generally I believe it's best to throw questions out and allow the Spirit to prompt individuals to answer. If you have a number of shy members, however, it may help to choose one or two questions from the guide and ask for a brief response from everyone. Anyone who doesn't want to respond can simply say "Pass."

At first I was hesitant to put individuals on the spot, but I have learned that many quiet people want you to do just that. They have things to say but they simply can't summon up the courage.

Sometimes, either in memory work or in answers to the same question, people are concerned about being repetitive. Repetition, however, may be the way the Spirit drums a point home.

4. Curtail the monopolizer. A person who talks too much is usually a person with special needs who can easily be hurt. Yet, no one should be answering nearly every question. Most people need a little time to think and to speak up. What if a monopolizer already has the floor?

As you are leading, ask to hear from those who haven't yet spoken. Or you might read aloud the advice of Carolyn Nystrom's studyguide on Romans:

> Decide if you are a talker or a listener . . . If you are a talker, before you speak count ten after the leader asks the question. Try waiting

until several other people speak before you give your own point of view. If you're a listener, remind yourself that just as you benefit from what others say, they profit from your ideas.[3]

If you still have a monopolizer, pray and be patient. Sometimes, when people first join a study, they talk a lot in order to make their identity known. As they feel more a part of the group, as they feel accepted, they'll talk less. Pray for the group to be accepting and loving.

5. *Encourage honesty by being honest.* Tell about your struggles. Make yourself vulnerable. If you as discussion leader admit your weaknesses, it will be easier for others to admit theirs.

Achieving such openness takes trust and time. One discussion leader complained to me that her group was not sharing openly. I asked her if she was making herself vulnerable. She told me that the week before she had confessed to the group her weakest area and her need for growth. The group had just stared at her silently. "I was bleeding and they were just watching!" she said. I encouraged her to pray and wait. Two meetings later, several women in the group opened up their inner selves and from then on the group began sharing heart to heart.

6. *Pray for individuals' concerns.* Some Bible study leaders don't allow for a "prayer and share" time because it cuts too deeply into the study time, a legitimate concern. Some groups never study: they just share.

I have found that it is possible to have controlled sharing. One simple solution is to study first and allow time for sharing during the last fifteen or thirty minutes. How sad if a person comes to the study carrying a burden and leaves with no relief. We are supposed to bear one another's burdens. I talked to one woman who dropped out of a group because, she explained,

I was having serious problems with my teenage daughter—we'd had a terrible fight that very morning. I was so upset I considered staying home—but I went to the study, hoping to get some support.

Near the end of the study I tried to share something about Jessie . . . the leader interrupted me and said she was sorry but they just couldn't take time for personal problems. I never went back. The leader called me later, but I'm not interested in Bible studies anymore. I think there's more warmth at The League of Women Voters!

I contrast that woman's experience with an experience I had in the first study I attended as a new Christian. Steve and I had just moved our family across the country, and he was doing a ninety-hour-a-week internship. I was having a rough time adjusting to his absence and to being so far from family and friends. When I heard about a young mothers' Bible study, I thought it might be the answer. At the end of the study the woman in charge asked if there were any needs they should know about. As I heard the women sharing I gathered the courage to speak up, but tears prevented me from finishing (I couldn't believe I was crying in front of a group of strangers). The leader asked if a few women would pray for me. For the next few minutes they enveloped me in prayer, and they didn't seem like strangers anymore. It didn't take much time, but it made the greatest difference to me.

A time of sharing personal needs isn't important only to women, it is just as important to men. Don Kimberlin, an area director for Inter-Varsity, explains,

To develop community, a group needs to spend some time each week sharing attitudes, problems, pains, frustrations, and joys . . . We all want someone to hear us in our walk with Christ. We get enough put-downs during the week from our bosses or our kids at home to numb our self-confidence. The community experience through small groups can be refreshing.[4]

People are drawn to groups not just by the power of the Word, but by the love and support they receive. The Scripture warns that even if we can fathom all mysteries and all knowledge, if we don't have love, we are nothing (1 Cor. 13:2). One of the best ways to express love is by sharing needs and agreeing to pray for one another.

If your group meets for an hour and a half or more, you have time for five or ten minutes of conversational prayer. The idea of praying out loud can strike terror in the heart of someone new to Bible study. So start slowly, perhaps with simple thank-you prayers. Let them know they don't have to speak out loud unless they want to. Teach them to pray conversationally. Conversational prayer consists of short sentences. Take one subject at a time. Then after several have prayed about that subject, move on to the next subject. For example:

Joe: Please be with me in my job interview tomorrow.
Vicky: Yes, Lord. If this is the job you want for Joe, please help him to get it.
Pete: Calm Joe's nerves—grant him the assurance that you are with him.
Joe: Yes, Lord! I agree with Vicky and Pete's prayers.

Vicky: Father, I want to thank you for providing for my financial needs.
Pete: We praise you that you are a God who answers prayer.

Once individuals discover they are not expected to deliver a lengthy monologue filled with *thee* and *thou,* they will begin to feel at ease about praying. Keep stressing the importance of short sentences or there may be a few whose dissertations will frighten everyone into silence. Rocky told me:

When I realized these guys were actually going to pray together I wanted to clear out. But after a couple of sessions, that was the part of the study that meant the most to me. It's harder for guys to open up—but boy, we need it just as much. Maybe more.

In addition to praying for one another and encouraging one another, we need to love "with actions and in truth" (1 John 3:18b). One morning in our study group Lorinda, usually buoyant, was weepy. Everything had piled up on her: exams, a messy house, and company arriving for dinner that evening. The group responded not just through prayer but by quickly organizing a plan for bringing in dinner.

7. *Divide and multiply.* If your attendance is consistently over fourteen, you're ready to divide. This is painful, but will bear much fruit. One group in Overton, Nebraska, began dividing by separating the rural women from the in-town women. Now they've grown to 80 women. Every September they put all the names in a hat and draw out ten names for each group.

Try This:

● Pray. Phone. Pray. Call each of the people in your group for the first few weeks. Let them know you appreciated having them there. Remind them of the time and place of the next meeting. After you hang up, pray specifically for that person.

● Subscribe to *The Fisherman's Net,* a resource quarterly with ideas to make your group better. It's free if you're a Bible study discussion leader. Write: The Fisherman's Net, Harold Shaw Publishers, Box 567, Wheaton, Illinois 60189.

Part III

Keeping

*Keeping: Teaching those
who seem to believe
to obey all
that Jesus commanded*

13
Disciple-Making

*One cannot separate evangelism and cultivation
and be true to the Biblical mandate.*
—James Engel[1]

*After Tom led me to Christ I felt as if I had a
salvation certificate in my pocket—I was "in." But Tom
wanted to keep meeting with me. At first I grumbled.
I thought, "Boy, this guy is sure going after me. I don't know
if I like this." But you know, there are umpteen
Christians who have known the Lord for years and still are
hardly able to feed themselves from the Word.
Tom's personal discipling changed my life.*
—Mike, a fruitful and dynamic Christian

WE MUST STOP SEEING conversion and discipleship as two steps. As long as we see first one and then the other, discipleship will be secondary. And secondary things are often left undone. In our limited vision, it is difficult to tell when someone is actually in the kingdom. Jesus knew that—and told the parable of the wheat and tares (Matt. 13:24-30). We must work with those who "seem to believe," not stopping when we think someone is converted.

Why Do We Make Disciples?
Jesus said: "Therefore go and make disciples of all nations, baptizing them in the name of the Father and of the Son and of the Holy Spirit, and teaching them to obey everything I have commanded you" (Matt. 28:19-20). Jesus never commanded

us to make converts; He said to make disciples. We are not to be satisfied until we have disciples.

The Greek word for *disciple* denotes a pupil who is adhering to the words of a teacher. When Jesus said "teach them to obey all I have commanded," He was saying, literally, "teach them to *keep* all I have commanded." We are not to be satisfied until we have taught those who seem to believe to keep all that Jesus commanded. As long as we don't see discipleship as an integral part of evangelism, those whom we think are won may not be won at all, and those who are won may never be strong enough to win others.

Bud, for example, told me he had fooled everyone in his church into thinking he had committed his life to Christ. One day his pastor came to pray with him about some business problems Bud was having. After he left, Bud thought, "Well, I've fooled my pastor, my friends, even my wife—but I can't fool God."

In the parable of the sower, three out of the four soils that received the Word never grew to fruit-bearing maturity. Three out of four seedlings died. If a gardener had a patch of strawberry plants and abandoned them as soon as he saw the tender green shoots poking out of the ground, what would happen? Because of neglect, most would wither and die. A wise gardener rejoices over the blades of green but continues right on working. Even if an individual "receives the Word with joy" (Mark 4:16b), we should keep on working until they are keeping that Word they received so positively.

Further, let's say that that strawberry plant lives, despite neglect. Will it ever be the kind of plant that will reproduce itself? Probably not. So the gardener's labor produces one season of fruit. That is good, but how much better if the gardener had nurtured that plant until it was strong enough to produce season after season.

James Engel has explained that as long as we see Christian growth as a second step, conversion will have center stage and the result will be a weakened church. God did not intend "to have His Kingdom occupied by vast numbers of spiritual babies,"[2] yet often our churches are filled with babies still living on milk, hearing the elementary truths of God's Word again and again. God's people should be moving on to solid food, feeding themselves and feeding others.

We should be a "peculiar" people. Instead we are barely distinguishable from the world. Like the world, we are often materialistic, uncaring, and impotent.

Discipleship belongs on center stage. We should not consider our friends to be fully won until they are disciples.

Vision for Multiplication

Do you remember the story of the Akron Bible study told at the beginning of this book? After a year of seeking the lost, we began our study with seven women. Without a vision for multiplication, that number could seem small and discouraging. But those women were our *base*. We wanted that base to be sturdy because it was going to support a superstructure. Six years later, those seven women had multiplied to forty-eight. As Leroy Eims, International Ministry Representative for The Navigators, says:

> Without a real vision of the power of multiplication, a man will not stick with another person through thick and thin. But when he can look into the face of this other person and see in it the whole world and the potential of reaching it for Christ, his enthusiasm is fired up by the Spirit of God who keeps him motivated and dynamically alive.[3]

In order to make disciples, to teach people to keep all that Jesus commanded, we need to be willing to commit ourselves to spending time and energy with just a few people. If we try to take on too many people in too short a time, we fail to build a sturdy base. Jesus worked closely with twelve men—He was building a base—and from those twelve came all of Christendom.

Leroy Eims tells of a conversation he had with a veteran

foreign missionary. This man told Leroy he felt he had wasted the last fifteen years of his life because he had failed to grasp the vision for multiplication. He compared his ministry to the approach of a man named Johnny:

> Johnny was a committed disciple of Jesus Christ, but he was going about his ministry in all the wrong ways, it seemed. In contrast to the typical missionary approach of the time, Johnny was spending the bulk of his time meeting with a few young men in that country.

The veteran missionary told Leroy he had tried to straighten Johnny out, but Johnny persisted in working with just a few. Fifteen years passed and the veteran missionary was about to return home. As he compared the fruit of his ministry with the fruit of Johnny's ministry, he told Leroy:

> I've got little to show for my time there. Oh, there is a group of people who meet in our assembly, but I wonder what will happen to them when I leave. They are not disciples. They have been faithful in listening to my sermons, but they do not witness. Few of them know how to lead another person to Christ. They know nothing about discipling others. And now that I am leaving, I can see I've all but wasted my time here.
>
> Then I look at what has come out of Johnny's life. One of the men he worked with is now a university professor whom God has used to reach and train scores of university students. Another is leading a witnessing and discipling team of about forty young men and women. Another is in a nearby city with a group of thirty-five growing disciples around him. Three have gone to other countries as missionaries and are now leading teams in those lands who are multiplying disciples. God is blessing their work.
>
> I see the contrast between my life and his and it is tragic. I was so sure I was right. What he was doing seemed so insignificant, but now I look at the results and they are staggering.[4]

All Christians want their lives to count for the Lord. We want to be like the good soil which "produced a crop, *multiplying,* thirty, sixty, or even a hundred times" (Mark 4:8). That can happen if we follow the example of Jesus.

Me? You? Disciples?

Dawson Trotman was founder of The Navigators. The Lord gave him a vision of the vast difference between being someone who would hear and receive the Word and being someone who would go on to train others. Embedded in The Navigators' philosophy is this scriptural imperative: "And the things you have heard me say in the presence of many witnesses entrust to reliable men who will also be qualified to teach others" (2 Tim. 2:2).

Dawson Trotman prayed for reliable and faithful men who would be qualified to teach others, and who would teach them to teach others. Scribbled in the margin of his Bible was the plea "That God will soon bring us into touch with a mighty band of young men, strong rugged soldiers of the cross, with an eye singled to His glory."⁵

How should you decide whom to disciple? Begin with prayer.

1. Pray. Be still before the Lord and ask Him for wisdom about whom to disciple. Jesus said His disciples were given to Him by the Father. Pray for discernment.

2. Choose someone who is committed. Choose someone who is faithful, reliable. Choose someone who will, because of his or her commitment, be likely to go on to train others. Jesus' disciples were varied, but they had one common trait: they left everything immediately to follow Him.

Steve and I have experienced the frustration of discipling (or trying to disciple) someone who is halfhearted in commitment to Christ. Though the time we spent was not in vain, there was little hope of future multiplication. In contrast, right now I am discipling a few young women who are already talking about whom they might disciple next year. The difference? They are committed.

Don't feel you *must* choose a brand-new Christian. Many persons who received Christ years ago would benefit greatly by going through a discipling program. What is lacking in their lives is not commitment but knowhow to train others.

3. Consider first those of your own sex. This isn't a hard and

fast rule—there are those who have been effectively discipled
by someone of the opposite sex—but it is a prudent consid-
eration. I have seen married women nearly wreck their homes
because they convinced themselves that the time they were
spending in the company of a single man was "discipling time."
By staying with one's own sex, there's less danger of temptation, less danger of misunderstanding. You are also more likely
to have similar life circumstances. Note that Paul told the older
women to train the younger women (Titus 2:3-5).

If you do lead someone of the opposite sex to the Lord, you
may wish to disciple him or her yourself. An alternative is to ask
another Christian to disciple him. Marge led Gordon to the Lord
but she didn't date him seriously until he had been thoroughly
discipled by a friend of hers. I enjoyed Gordon's description of
his first encounter with Warf, his discipler:

> Shortly after I had prayed with Marge to receive Christ, she told me
> she had someone she wanted me to meet. We parked the car about
> a block away from his basement apartment. It was raining hard and
> we ran all the way and pounded on the door. Warf threw open the
> door and welcomed us inside magnanimously. Marge introduced
> us and he shook my hand vigorously, saying it was wonderful to
> meet a new brother in the Lord. Before I knew it, Marge was gone
> and Warf was telling me to take off my coat and sit down at the
> table. He handed me an index card with a Scripture verse on it. He
> told me to sit down and meditate on that while he fixed us some
> fresh coffee. I had never meditated on a verse in my life, but I
> started that night.

Warf trained Gordon and Gordon went on to train others. And
Gordon and Marge were married four years later.

4. Concentrate on a few. To concentrate on a few is an
important lesson. If you spread yourself too thin, you will fail.
You may minister to many individuals in your life, as Jesus did,
but you should concentrate on molding just a few, as Jesus did.
A few at a time, over a lifetime, multiplied by a few at a time,
over their lifetimes, will result in great things for God.

How Do You Make Disciples?

How did Jesus disciple His men? He chose a few and spent time with them. He embodied the instructions given in Deuteronomy 6:5-7:

> "Love the Lord your God with all your heart and with all your soul and with all your strength. These commandments that I give you today are to be on your hearts. Impress them on your children. Talk about them when you sit at home and when you walk along the road, when you lie down and when you get up."

For three intensive years, as he sat with them in the homes of friends, as he walked with them along the sea of Galilee, Jesus taught his disciples. He taught them not only in word but in deed. They watched Him as He showed compassion for the lost, the sick, and the despised. Day in and day out they were with Him, listening and watching, until they became like Him.

Simple? Yes. Easy? No. Making disciples is not complicated, but it takes commitment. Shortcuts will fail.

Jesus met with His disciples in a formal way. He told them about the Lord's commandments, He explained His parables, He taught them how to pray. We too must meet with our disciples formally, teaching them until they can teach others.

It helps to have a plan. I use The Navigator Wheel shown in figure 7 (p. 166) as a basis for my plan.[6]

If I could add a fifth spoke to this wheel it would be ministry. The Spirit has gifted each believer uniquely and part of obedience is discovering that gift and putting it to use in a specific ministry.

A Spirit-filled Christian focuses on Christ and is concerned about the Word, fellowship, prayer, witnessing, and developing a ministry.

John, now in full-time Christian service, was discipled by Dwayne. He told me that the impact those months had on his life was tremendous.

> Dwayne helped me develop a solid devotional life. He'd check me up on that, ask me how I was doing it—and he'd share how he was

doing it. When I'd see him he'd tell me the things God had been teaching him in his quiet times. I began to realize that my devotional time was not just an exercise but a time of really seeking God. Dwayne showed me how to discover truths from Scripture and not go off on tangents. He would pray with me. We both had friends we wanted to influence for the Lord, so we'd pray for them. He taught me how to prepare an effective three-minute testimony.

Figure 7

The Word
In the group I am discipling now, we are going through 1 John. I assign passages in segments (usually a chapter or less) and ask them to write, in a notebook:

1. Facts
2. Meaning
3. Application

It's wise to use a modern translation of the Bible, and keep a notebook. Writing down what we learn helps us to dig, not just read. It forces us to stay alert, continually seeking the Lord's message and articulating it in our own words. Keeping a notebook is the key to a vital devotional life.⁷ If you teach someone to keep a notebook you go beyond feeding them to teaching them to eat.

I also assign memory verses to the person I'm discipling. An effective technique in memorizing a verse is to take it word by word instead of phrase by phrase. While that may seem slower, it actually is faster because you learn it word-perfect and there's less need to backtrack. For example, to memorize 1 John 2:15, you would say:

1
1 John
1 John 2
1 John 2:15
1 John 2:15 Love
1 John 2:15 Love not
1 John 2:15 Love not the
1 John 2:15 Love not the world
etc.

End by repeating the reference, to keep it firmly in your mind.

Marilyn told me that, as a new Christian, she tended to doubt her salvation. She was given some verses on *assurance* to memorize, which she did. "They kept coming back to me during those times of doubt, reminding me that I was indeed His," she explained.

So often we think of memorization as helping us prepare a clear witness. I don't want to minimize that, but it's also important to choose verses that will help us overcome sin and lead a victorious life. Our goal is to teach those we are discipling to be obedient, to be keepers of the Word. People may balk at memory work, but once they've begun to do it they will discover that it is a key to unleashing power in their spiritual life. Lydia told me:

> What a delight it is to have God's great thoughts moving around in my head, popping out at "odd" and also relevant times. Once again I am humbled by the Lord's reminder that the disciplines I avoid are delights that He longs to share with me.

Mike told me that at first he felt scared and reluctant to begin the disciplined program his friend was encouraging. But memorization gave him power. "God worked through the Scriptures and changed my life."

In my present group I assign two or three verses a week—we all do the same ones. I ask them to meditate on them during the week, turning them over and over seeking new insights.

Witnessing
Help your friend to present the gospel clearly and to give a brief but meaningful testimony. Campus Crusade pairs off their workers and asks them to practice, practice, practice!

Of course, it's not enough to be prepared to share our faith, we must do it. One week in my group we each were to invite a non-Christian friend to something—a Bible study, a gospel concert, lunch. It's exciting to hear the reports of assignments in this area.

Mike told me, "There's nothing that helps you grow like being on the battlefield sharing your faith. I'm challenged to know God and who He is by the questions people ask me."

Prayer
Learning to use a notebook for prayer is helpful. Write down prayer requests, making them as specific as possible. A prayer notebook allows you to check over past requests, marking them with arrows (faith-strengthening arrows) as they are answered.

One idea is to pray for some things every day (praise, confession, commitment, family) and some things once a week (neighbors on Monday, missionaries on Tuesday, etc.).

Training another person is bound to strengthen you. The other day after Bible study as I dropped Shell off, she turned to me before closing the car door and asked, "How much time do you spend in prayer each day?" Her question convicted me and I rededicated myself to shaping up what was becoming a rather sloppy prayer life.

Diane told me that Shannon showed her how to do a topical

study on prayer using a concordance. Shannon also gave Diane a couple of books on prayer. *"What Happens When Women Pray* is the book that challenged me to develop a disciplined prayer life," she said.

Books

Pray for discernment as you recommend books. Melissa moaned, "I was given books all right! The wrong books. They were so difficult, all loaded with doctrine my mind couldn't begin to grasp. I felt like giving up." When you choose books, ask the Lord to help you remember which ones were most helpful to you as a beginning student. "Books should be given like a prescription," one man advised. "They should be chosen to tailor-fit that person's need, intellect, and interests."

Fellowship

Jesus' actions gave His words substance. He embodied the Word He spoke.

We must be keepers of the Word ourselves in order to teach others to be keepers of the Word. Paul said, "Whatever you have learned or received or heard from me, or *seen in me*—put it into practice" (Phil. 4:9). By inviting those whom we are discipling to go along with us as we teach a children's Bible club, visit a sick friend, or take our children swimming, we are giving them a chance to be discipled informally. That kind of closeness helps others to see us as we reflect Him, however dimly.

When I was less than a year old in Christ, Shirley, a friend from Indianapolis, invited me to her house for lunch. I watched her intently as she dealt with her children. When her little girl slammed the door as she came in, Shirley lovingly but firmly told her to come in again and close the door the right way. I had always been told to "Praise the good and ignore the bad in children" and consequently my son was wild. I also recall Shirley's telling her children that soon God was going to make the apples in the trees sweet and ripe and we'd all be able to drink apple cider. Shirley was training me that day, through fellowship, to be a godly mother.

Margie became a Christian through the influence of Tom when she was living in Hawaii. She told me about the impact fellowshiping with him had on her life:

> We used to hike around the Island. Sometimes we'd ride bikes, sometimes we'd take a picnic. Tom's heart was so full of the Lord, it just overflowed into natural conversation. He also took me to his church and introduced me to his friends. Tom cared about all kinds of people in a way I'd never seen anyone care. He cared about me. He cared about my walk with the Lord.

The last time I talked to Margie she was on her way to Cambodia to work with World Concern. She had become like the one with whom she spent time.

Spending time with a new Christian informally gives you a chance to answer all the questions that come to their mind during Bible study but which might lead the group off on tangents. It also provides an opportunity to talk privately about areas in their life where they are struggling. Tracy said of Lee,

> She continually encouraged me to look at myself and my priorities or goals. She was very open to my struggles, honest in dealing with them, and almost more patient than Job.

Ministry

The one you disciple will watch you developing the gifts God has given you. They will also see what fulfillment you receive through obeying God in this way.

One young woman told me that before she began her children's Bible club she was depressed within herself. After she started using this gift her attitude became so positive that she began each week excited about what good things would happen. "It's so important," she said, "to get out there and serve."

Point out to your friend the wide range of possibilities for ministry. One individual might use his gift of evangelism with college students, another her gift of administration in a local food bank, and another his gift of mercy in nursing home visitation. Encourage your disciple to consider first a ministry in the fertile field.

Results of Discipling Someone

Discipling bears fruit. It turns ordinary Christians into extraordinary ones. Sue told me that although she received the Lord when she was seven years old, she wasn't discipled until she was twenty-two.

> My husband and I were at Travis Air Force Base when a couple from The Navigators asked if they could meet with us as a couple in order to disciple us. It was during that time that I realized Jesus had to be Lord of my life in every aspect—I had to give myself to Him totally.

As a result of formal discipling, Sue and her husband Wayne began leading fruitful lives. They have adopted two Korean orphans, and Sue does day care at home where she says she can "teach and show the children the love of Jesus."

Try This:

● Give yourself a vision for discipleship by reading the biography of Dawson Trotman, founder of The Navigators: *Daws,* by Betty Lee Skinner (Zondervan).

● Do you have children at home? They are clearcut choices for discipling. Choose a biblical proverb a week and memorize it as a family. Act it out, discuss it, seek ways to apply it. One day your children will be teaching this proverb to their children.

● Call and invite the person or persons the Lord has placed on your heart to take part in a discipleship program. Go through Book 1 in The Navigator's Discipleship Series *(Your Life in Christ).* Make it clear that you must meet together regularly and do memory work.

14
Wake Up!

Wake up! Strengthen what remains and is about to die,
for I have not found your deeds complete in
the sight of my God. Remember, therefore, what you have
received and heard; obey it and repent. But if
you do not wake up, I will come like a thief, and you will
not know at what time I will come to you.
—Revelation 3:2

WHEN I CAME TO THE LORD, He turned my life around. He gave
me,

"a crown of beauty
instead of ashes,
the oil of gladness
instead of mourning,
and a garment of praise
instead of a spirit of despair."
(Isa. 61:3)

Steve and I began attending an evangelistic church, and I felt
these were the most wonderful people I'd ever met. I still do.

And yet, I am now aware that, sixteen years later, all is not as
it seems—in my life, or in the lives of my brothers and sisters in
Christ. It is possible, even common, for us who pride ourselves

on knowing God's Word to be only apparently spiritual. We are like the church at Sardis in the book of Revelation. We have some strength, but we are sleeping. We need to wake up, remember what we have received and heard, keep on keeping that Word, and repent.

True Spirituality

It is possible to know the right doctrines, to use the right terminology, even to be having regular quiet times, yet be only superficially spiritual. This is the kind of person the Lord confronts in Isaiah 58.

On the outside (v. 2), these people "seemed eager to know God's ways." They also had regular "quiet times": "day after day they seek me out." They seemed to be doing what was right. It seemed as if they had "not forsaken the commands of ... God." Had these people had Bibles, they would have been full of yellow underlinings and notes scribbled in the margins. These people even practiced the discipline of fasting.

But God could see their hearts, and He knew that their hearts were far from Him. He said, "On the day of your fasting, 'you do as you please' " (v. 3). It is possible for us to appear to be walking closely with Him, even to think we are walking with Him, and yet to be deceiving ourselves, to be slipping back into living for ourselves. True spirituality means no longer living for ourselves, but for Him who died for us and was raised again (2 Cor. 5:15). True spirituality means strengthening ourselves with the Word, prayer, and fellowship in order to go out into the world and become involved with those in spiritual and physical need.

Greg Scharf, pastor and author, has said:

> The besetting sin of evangelicals is that we have redefined obedience in our own terms instead of God's terms. We have limited it simply to the things we are already doing, to "church things" rather than including all kinds of other things.

Too often Christians feel they are spiritual if they are involved in church activities. But unless they are injecting themselves into the brokenness of people's lives, they are only apparently spiritual.

Isaiah tells us that true spirituality means "Share your food with the hungry and bring right into your own homes those who are helpless, poor and destitute. Clothe those who are cold and don't hide from relatives who need your help. Feed the hungry! Help those in trouble!" (Isa. 58:7, 10 TLB).

We have turned our backs on a hungry world. Millions of people starve every year, but we have convinced ourselves that we are obeying the Lord because we are busy in church. The gospel means we will be concerned about people physically, emotionally, and spiritually. We can't separate one from the other and call ourselves compassionate. When people are hungry or unfairly treated or hurting, we, as Christ's ambassadors, must find creative ways of bearing their burdens. Perhaps when we love whole persons and inject ourselves into their lives, they will listen with hearing ears to the gospel of Jesus Christ.

Isaiah tells us we are to "set the oppressed free and break every yoke" (Isa. 58:6). Jesus said He came to "preach good news to the poor . . . and . . . to release the oppressed" (Luke 4:18). Don't let's lull ourselves into thinking we are obeying when what we have really done is redefined obedience in our own terms. We must wake up, "call to mind the lessons we have received and heard; continually lay them to heart and obey them, and repent" (Rev. 3:3 AMPLIFIED)! Isaiah concludes his stern warning with a promise:

> "If you do away with the yoke of oppression,
> with the pointing finger and malicious talk,
> and if you spend yourselves on behalf of the hungry,
> and satisfy the needs of the oppressed,
> then your light will rise in the darkness,
> and your night will become like the noonday.

The Lord will guide you always;
he will satisfy your needs in a sun-scorched land
and will strengthen your frame.
You will be like a well-watered garden,
like a spring whose waters never fail"
(Isa. 58:9b-11).

NOTES

AKRON—AN OVERVIEW

1. James Engel, *Contemporary Christian Communications* (Nashville: Thomas Nelson, 1979), p. 166.
2. Michel Eyquem de Montaigne, "Apology for Raimond de Seborde," *Essays of Montaigne,* trans. Charles Cotton, Vol. 3, Book 2 (London, Navarre Society, 1923), p. 162.
3. James Engel, pp. 66-67.

1/JESUS MAKES A DIFFERENCE

1. Paul E. Little, *How to Give Away Your Faith,* cassette 1 (Costa Mesa, Calif.: One Way Library, 1973).
2. J. I. Packer, *Knowing God* (Downers Grove, Ill.: InterVarsity Press, 1973), p. 134.
3. *Ibid.,* p. 136.
4. Reprinted from *Christianity Today,* October 11, 1974. Copyright © 1974 by *Christianity Today.* Used by permission.
5. Em Griffin, "Winning Over—How to Change People's Minds," *Eternity,* May 1976, p. 28.

2/ECCLESIASTES PRESENT-TENSE

1. Dee Brestin, *Ecclesiastes: God's Wisdom for Evangelism,* A Fisherman Bible Studyguide (Wheaton, Ill.: Harold Shaw Publishers, 1980), p. 12.
2. Gail Sheehy, *Passages* (New York: E. P. Dutton and Co., 1974), p. 6.

3/FINDING TIME FOR OTHERS

1. James Dobson, "A Man and His Work," *Straight Talk to Men and Their Wives* Session 5, Tape 3 (Waco, Tex.: Word Educational Products Division, 1980).
2. Dorothy Pape, *In Search of God's Ideal Woman* (Downers Grove, Ill.: InterVarsity Press, 1976), p. 346.
3. Doris Longacre, *Living More With Less* (Scottdale, Pa.: Herald Press, 1980), p. 171.

4. Charles Hummel, *Tyranny of the Urgent* (Downers Grove, Ill.: InterVarsity Press, 1967), pp. 7-8, 11.

4/SEEING THE PEOPLE IN YOUR PATH

1. Vance Packard, *A Nation of Strangers* (New York: Pocket Books, 1974), p. 146.
2. Keith Miller, *The Taste of New Wine* (Waco, Tex.: Word Books, 1965), p. 93.
3. Alan Loy McGinniss, *The Friendship Factor* (Minneapolis: Augsburg, 1979), p. 54.
4. Karen Burton Mains, *Open Heart—Open Home* (Elgin, Ill.: David C. Cook, 1976), p. 135.
5. B. J. Thomas, "B. J. Thomas in Concert" cassette, (Universal City: MCA Records, 1980).
6. McGinniss, p. 54.

5/THE FERTILE FIELD

1. Engel, *Contemporary Christian Communications,* p. 120.
2. *Ibid.,* p. 121.
3. *Ibid.,* p. 117.
4. "Message," *Multnomah School of the Bible News,* March-April 1982, p. 1.
5. Herman H. ter Welle, "Evangelization of Children," *Let The Earth Hear His Voice* (Minneapolis: World Wide Publications, 1975), p. 725.
6. Child Evangelism Fellowship has a helpful magazine, *Evangelizing Today's Child.* For a subscription write to P.O. Box 348, Warrenton, Missouri 63383.
7. Josh McDowell, "No Joshing... He's Number One," *Worldwide Challenge,* September 1980, p. 7.
8. If you wish to be on the mailing list, write: International Students, Inc., Star Ranch, P.O. Box C, Colorado Springs, Colorado 80901.

178

Notes

9. *Doorways,* International Students, Inc. Volume 6, Number 2, p. 1.
10. The address for InterCristo is P.O. Box 33487, Seattle, Washington 98133. Their toll-free number is (800) 426-1342.

6/SATAN'S SCHEMES

1. Em Griffin, *The Mind Changers* (Wheaton, Ill.: Tyndale House, 1976), p. 6.
2. John Stott, *Christian Mission in the Modern World* (Downers Grove, Ill.: InterVarsity Press, 1975), p. 81.
3. *Ibid.*
4. *Ibid.*
5. Engel, *Contemporary Christian Communications,* p. 196.
6. *Alcohol Effects Series* (Lincoln, Neb.: Nebraska Division on Alcoholism, 1980).
7. *Ibid.*
8. Paul Beeson, M.D. et al., eds., *Textbook of Medicine* (Philadelphia: W. B. Saunders, 1979), p. 707.
9. *Ibid.*
10. Griffin, p. 6.
11. It is often overlooked that thousands of evangelical women (and some evangelical men) describe themselves as "biblical feminists" or "evangelical feminists." Some are members of the national Evangelical Women's Caucus, P.O. Box 3192, San Francisco, CA 94119.
12. "Getting Ahead," *Ladies Home Journal,* May 1980, p. 48.
13. Erica Diamond, "A Fascinating Woman Gets Sprung or If Marabel Could Only See Me Now," *Free Indeed,* December/January 1978/79, p. 11.
14. Marabel Morgan, *The Total Woman* (New York: Pocket Books, 1975), p. 60.
15. *Ibid.,* p. 96.
16. "Fighting the Housewife Blues," *Time Magazine,* 14 March 1977, p. 3.
17. *Ibid.*

18. "Safety, Shelter, Rules, Form, Love —The Promise of the Ultra-Right," *Ms. Magazine,* June 1979, p. 64.
19. Letters to the Editor, *Moody Monthly,* July 1975.

7/A LIFE WITH A MESSAGE

1. Rebecca Manley Pippert, *Out of the Saltshaker and into the World* (Downers Grove, Ill.: InterVarsity Press, 1979), p. 24.
2. Jim Petersen, *Evangelism as a Lifestyle* (Colorado Springs: NavPress, 1980), p. 108.
3. Arthur McPhee, *Friendship Evangelism* (Grand Rapids: Zondervan, 1978), p. 44.
4. Pippert, p. 24.
5. Paul Little, *How to Give Away Your Faith,* cassette 3 (Costa Mesa, Calif.: One Way Library, 1973).
6. George Gallup, "What We Know and What We Do Not Know About Evangelizing 80 Million Unchurched Americans," *New Catholic World,* July/August 1976, p. 149.
7. "The Outsiders," *Eternity,* January 1980, p. 22.
8. Gallup, p. 149.
9. "Brief Case," *Eternity,* September 1982, p. 13.
10. W. E. Vine, *Expository Dictionary of New Testament Words* (Old Tappan, N. J.: Revell, 1940), p. 116.
11. Tom Rees, *World Congress on Evangelism,* Volume 2 (Minneapolis: World Wide Publications, 1967).

8/PREPARING YOURSELF

1. J. I. Packer, *Evangelism and the Sovereignty of God* (Leicester, England: Inter-Varsity Press, 1961), p. 87.

9/ENCOURAGING A RESPONSE

1. Paul Little, *How to Give Away Your Faith,* cassette series, (Costa Mesa, Calif.: One Way Library, 1973).

2. Packer, *Evangelism and the Sovereignty of God,* p. 122.
3. Petersen, *Evangelism as a Lifestyle,* p. 107.
4. *Doorways,* Vol. 6, No. 2, p. 4.

10/CONVERSION: A PROCESS
1. Packer, *Evangelism and the Sovereignty of God,* pp. 121 & 123.
2. Elisabeth Elliot, *Shadow of the Almighty* (New York: Harper & Brothers, 1958), p. 78.
3. Engel, *Contemporary Christian Communications,* p. 146.
4. Packer, p. 119.
5. Howard Hendricks, *Say It With Love* (Wheaton, Ill.: Victor Books, 1972), p. 51.

11/WAYS TO REACH OUT
1. "Mass Evangelism: The Bottom Line" *Eternity,* September 1977.
2. Naomi Wright, *An Ever-Widening Circle* (Portland, Ore.: Multnomah Press, 1977), p. 84.
3. C. S. Lewis, *Reflections on the Psalms* (New York: Harcourt, Brace, & World, Inc., 1958), p. 1-2.
4. Joseph Bayly, *The Gospel Blimp* (Grand Rapids: Zondervan, 1960).
5. Martha Reapsome, "How to Start an Inductive Bible Study," *The Fisherman's Net* (Harold Shaw Publishers), Vol. 1, No. 2, p. 1.

12/BIBLE STUDIES
1. Jim Petersen, *Evangelism as a Lifestyle,* p. 143.
2. *Ibid.*
3. Carolyn Nystrom, *A Woman's Workshop on Romans* (Grand Rapids: Zondervan, 1981), p. 10.
4. Don Kimberlin, "Power Comes in Small Packages," *The Fisherman's Net,* Vol. 2, No. 3, pp. 1, 3.

13/DISCIPLE-MAKING
1. Engel, *Contemporary Christian Communications,* p. 66.
2. *Ibid.,* p. 67.
3. Leroy Eims, *The Lost Art of Disciple Making* (Colorado Springs: NavPress, 1978), p. 85.
4. *Ibid.,* p. 23.
5. Betty Lee Skinner, *Daws* (Grand Rapids: Zondervan, 1974), p. 69.
6. From "The Spirit-filled Christian," Book 2 of the Design for Discipleship series. Copyright © 1973 by The Navigators. Published by NavPress, Colorado Springs, Colorado. Used by permission. All rights reserved.
7. Chuck and Winnie Christensen, *How To Listen When God Speaks* (Wheaton, Ill.: Harold Shaw Publishers, 1979).